D1361870

Tinker v. Des Moines

Student Protest

Leah Farish

Landmark Supreme Court Cases

Enslow Publishers, Inc.

44 Fadem Road   PO Box 38
Box 699   Aldershot
Springfield, NJ 07081   Hants GU12 6BP
USA   UK

To my parents, who allowed peaceful protest
but not substantial disruption.

Library of Congress Cataloging-in-Publication Data

Farish, Leah.
    Tinker v. Des Moines: student protest / Leah Farish.
        p. cm. — (Landmark Supreme Court cases)
    Includes bibliographical references and index.
    Summary: Considers the landmark case that dealt with the
rights of students to wear arm bands to protest U.S.
involvement in the Vietnam War.
    ISBN 0-89490-859-6
    1. Tinker, John Frederick—Trials, litigation, etc.—Juvenile literature.
2. Des Moines Independent Community School District—Trials,
litigation, etc.—Juvenile literature. 3. Freedom of speech—United States—
Juvenile literature. 4. Vietnamese Conflict, 1961-1975—Protest movements—
Iowa—Des Moines—Juvenile literature. [1. Tinker, John Frederick—Trials,
litigation, etc. 2. Freedom of speech. 3. Vietnamese Conflict, 1961-1975—
Protest movements. 4. Trials.] I. Title II. Series.
KF228.T56F37   1997
342.73'0853—dc20
[347.302853]
                                96-25704
                                CIP
                                AC

Printed in the United States of America.

10 9 8 7 6 5 4 3 2 1

Photo Credits: A/P Wide World Photos, p. 70; "Collection of the Supreme Court
of the United States.", p. 79; © Copyright Jennifer Ferranti, 1994, p. 101; *Des
Moines Register*, pp. 86, 106; Harris & Ewing, "Collection of the Supreme Court
of the United States.", p. 65; Leah Farish, ©1995, pp. 12, 21, 31; Lesley Rea, Tulsa,
Oklahoma, ©1995, p. 98; UPI/Bettman, p. 14; Yoichi R. Okamoto, LBJ Library,
pp. 8, 25, 40, 45, 51, 54.

Cover Photo: UPI/Bettman

Contents

1

A Matter of Conscience

It was December 11, 1965, and sixteen-year-old Christopher Eckhardt was shoveling snow out of the driveway. Christmas lights twinkled throughout his hometown of Des Moines, Iowa. When he finished his work, he walked back into his house, joining some people who were gathered there to talk about peace on earth. It does not sound like the beginning of a historic legal battle. But that is how it began.

Inside the house were some college students and others, including Mrs. Lorena Jeanne Tinker and Chris Eckhardt's mother, Margaret. Reverend Tinker arrived later. Mrs. Eckhardt was president of the city's chapter of the Women's International League for Peace and Freedom. As such, she had been extensively involved in protesting American involvement in the Vietnam War.

She and Christopher had, just two weeks before, participated in an antiwar march from the White House to the Washington Monument. One idea discussed at the Eckhardt's house was to wear black armbands from December 16 through New Year's Day, to make a silent plea for peace.[1]

The next night the Eckhardts hosted another meeting—this time for high school students. The theme was the same—the war and how to stop it. It was agreed that those attending would decide for themselves whether or not to wear the armbands.[2]

On the next Wednesday evening, two of the high school students interested in the protest visited the Tinker home. They brought copies of a paper titled "We Mourn." John Tinker, age fifteen, read it and agreed with it. John's parents and sister Mary Beth, age thirteen, discussed the issues, and John and Mary Beth decided to wear the armbands to school the next day. For them, it was an act of mourning the dead of both sides from the war, and an act of support for a truce, or end of fighting, in Vietnam. Senator Robert Kennedy, the brother of the late President John F. Kennedy, opposed the war and was urging that a Christmas truce, which had already been announced, should be changed to an indefinite truce. This might encourage the United States and their enemies in North Vietnam to negotiate. John Tinker said a few months later: "The idea of an indefinite truce was originally Robert Kennedy's and I hoped that such a truce would stop the killing and might lead to a peaceful settlement in the war. In addition to the wearing of the armbands there was going to be a fast on New Year's Eve and one other day and I did fast during those days."[3] First, the students phoned the president of the school board to work things out without conflict. "I thought that—you know—he could at least listen to us and hear what we were going to try to say."[4] But the president said no meetings with the school board could take place until the next regularly scheduled time, the following week. The young people were faced with a decision. Their consciences said to wear the armbands. Mary Beth adds, "This decision was my own, neither mother or father attempted to convince me. . . ."[5] Chris Eckhardt, too, headed for school the next day wearing an armband.

The problem was that the school had announced in the newspaper on December 15 that wearing these armbands was going to be against the rules: "For the good of the school system we don't think this should be permitted. The schools are no place for demonstrations. We allow for free discussion of these things in the classes . . . the educational program would be disturbed by students wearing armbands."[6]

Robert Kennedy proposed a truce in Vietnam. This was one of the things John Tinker supported by wearing his black armband.

Students at school had a variety of reactions. Mary Beth later said, "Everyone talks in homemaking class while we are sewing. The girls at my table told me I had better take it [the armband] off or I would get in trouble. They were not threatening me, they were just trying to keep me out of trouble."[7] John recalls that "some of the students were making fun of me for wearing it. . . .[s]ome of them didn't think I should do this, but they thought I should have the right to if I wanted to. . . . A football player named Joe Thompson told the kids to leave me alone; that everybody had their own opinions."[8] Mary Beth and John Tinker were asked to remove the bands and their parents were contacted. Reverend Tinker remembers, "I became convinced that this was very definitely a matter of conscience for them, that they were not lightly defying authority . . . but they had a conviction . . . and I had to make a choice as to whether or not I would stand by my children . . . I thought the school authorities had to obey the Constitution and I still do."[9] He was referring to his children's right to free speech and freedom of religion under the First Amendment, which says: "Congress shall make no law . . . prohibiting the free exercise [of religion]; or abridging [limiting] the freedom of speech, or of the press. . . ."

Reverend Tinker was an ordained Methodist

minister who had been a pastor. He had been appointed by his bishop to work for the American Friends Service Committee, which drew its name from the Society of Friends, or Quakers.[10] His children had exposure to Quaker beliefs, especially on the subject of war. Quakers, a branch of Christian religion, have a long tradition of pacifism, or opposition to warfare. They base this on Jesus's teaching that if we are struck on one cheek, we are to "turn the other cheek" rather than fight back.[11] John testified, "I have been in several demonstrations in the war and several Civil Rights demonstrations. The subject of peace and the subject of the war . . . are discussed quite often in my home. These are concerns which I share with my parents. . . . I attend a Friends meeting [church] and have been so attending for four years."[12] Many Quakers at the time were saying that "in the tragedy of war, our responsibility . . . is to engage in imaginative acts of peacemaking. . . ."[13] The wearing of armbands, fasting, sit-ins, and resistance to the draft were some of the pacifists' expressions of their beliefs.

John and Mary Beth's early background was not Quaker but Methodist. They heard their father when he preached. The Methodist denomination also taught that life was sacred and that people served a higher power than their government. Their father would no doubt have agreed when the General Conference of the United Methodist Church said: "We dedicate ourselves to peace throughout the world. . . ."[14]

The whole family was so committed to their beliefs that even their ten-year-old sister and eight-year-old brother wore armbands to school on December 16. Their mother recalls, "Hope came down the stairs with an armband, and her father said, 'Where are you going with that?' She said, 'Even though I'm only ten, I can grieve for the people who have died in Vietnam.' Her father said, 'People are going to say, "There go the Tinkers again."[15] But the excitement happened at the schools where Chris Eckhardt, and John and Mary Beth Tinker attended.

Chris decided to face his school authorities directly: "When I arrived at school with the armband on I went right to the Administrative Office after going to my locker because I knew I was breaking a rule. I didn't expect exactly to be suspended . . . I didn't know exactly what they would do."[16]

Mary Beth went to math class after lunch. She was circulating a petition to allow students "the right to wear any armband or crucifixes or anything like that."[17] Apparently this petition never interfered with class, because it never became an issue in the court case to come. So far there had been no disruption. Mr.

High school debaters in the Midwest prepare to debate the topic of the year in 1970—whether the United States should intervene in a war in a foreign country.

Moberly, her math teacher, had said earlier that ". . . if there was going to be a demonstration in my class, it would be for or against something in mathematics. . . . I had expressed my view on demonstrations that were against things and not for things. . . ."[18] When he saw her armband, he told Mary Beth to go to the principal's office. There, she removed her armband as requested, and returned to class. But the incident was not over.

Miss Vera Ann Tarmann, girls' advisor, appeared at Mary Beth's class, and accompanied her back to the office. Miss Tarmann said she personally sympathized with Mary Beth's opinions, and that she herself was a descendant of Quakers. But the advisor went on to say that Mary Beth must be suspended and could not return to school wearing an armband.[19]

The outcomes at John's and Chris's schools were similar. The school district's principals had planned for this, and the policy they had made public in the newspaper must be enforced.[20] The next school board meeting, held a few days later, was buzzing.

An official describes it: "Our board room was filled to overflowing. There were a few signs present and on several occasions it was a little bit touch-and-go as far as maintaining order, but we did get through."[21] Some of the people in attendance were of the view that "If you don't have discipline, you don't [sic] have

Mary Beth Tinker and her brother John display two black armbands. They were both suspended from classes with three other students for wearing the bands to mourn the Vietnam War dead.

anything."[22] But another of the suspended students, Bruce Clark, reminded the board that in 1963, students had been permitted to wear black armbands in mourning over an Alabama church bombing in which four African-American girls died.[23] According to Lorena Jeanne Tinker, some teachers came to their family afterwards and said that they had wanted to speak out for the protesting students, but they feared for their jobs.[24] It looked like the board might just postpone any decision, but Craig Sawyer, the attorney the students had asked to represent them at the meeting, called out, "Take a stand! That's what you're here for!"[25] The board kept in place the rule against armbands for the time being. No one was sure what the new year would bring.

2

Che 60s: A Cime of Love, Peace, and War

The *Tinker* case reached the Supreme Court in the 1960s. Historic events of that time were covered fully by the media as never before. The whole nation's attention was on these events, yet the country was divided in its reactions to them.

It was a decade when young people took a new place in public debate and influenced the course of events. The decade began with John F. Kennedy's election as president in November 1960. At forty-three, he was the youngest man elected president. In February of that year, four black teenagers protested discrimination by walking into a store in North Carolina, taking seats at the whites-only lunch counter, and asking to be served. Their polite refusal to leave started months of peaceful racial protest, often in the form of "sit-ins," in the area.[1]

President Kennedy's ". . . [a]dministration sparkled with ideas for a better and more constructive life for more people everywhere. Yet in most instances . . . [those ideas] had to await . . . his successor [Lyndon Johnson], who knew how to translate the Kennedy ideals and ideas into legislative reality—something which Kennedy had not generally mastered. On the other side of the . . . ledger, however, was the emerging involvement in Vietnam, for which the Kennedy Administration must share a very real measure of blame."[2]

How did we originally become involved in the war in Vietnam? Our long-time allies, the French, had colonies in the area before World War II, and after the Japanese were defeated, France wanted to reestablish its interests. But communist leader Ho Chi Minh organized opposition, and twenty-five thousand Frenchmen died in the fighting. France asked then-United States President Dwight Eisenhower to step in and help. Among those who spoke up against it were young senators John Kennedy and Lyndon Johnson.[3] The United States did not want to be further involved until the South Vietnamese had decided to fight communism themselves. Ho Chi Minh continued to dominate North Vietnam with communism, while in the South the noncommunist, but dictator-like, Ngo Dinh Diem ruled. So Eisenhower decided to offer military and financial help to Diem, in return for a promise that Diem would promote democracy in the land. This was called "the Eisenhower commitment." However, Diem's promised reforms never came.[4] In fact, persecutions of his enemies grew worse, and by 1960 the Vietcong, rebels against Diem encouraged by Ho Chi Minh, were angry enough to fight for communism.[5]

Kennedy did not favor our involvement in Vietnam, saying on television, "In the final analysis, it is their war [the Vietnamese people's] war."[6] But he hoped that by negotiations and sending more "advisers" and help to Diem, things would improve with time. But time was not on his side.[7] Kennedy was tragically assassinated on November 22, 1963.

Johnson filled the rest of Kennedy's term and was re-elected in 1964, in a time of prosperity and relative peace. "In the campaign year of 1964 Vietnam was not an issue of any significance. . . . [None of his speeches was primarily] devoted to the conflict in Southeast Asia."[8] What preoccupied Johnson were his domestic plans—the Economic Opportunities Act, the Food Stamp Act, the War on Poverty, federal funds and requirements directed to public schools, and the Civil Rights Act of 1964.[9] These ambitious programs were part of his vision for America, the "Great Society."

Johnson later said:

> I knew from the start that I was bound to be crucified either way I moved. If I left . . . the Great Society—in order to get involved with . . . a war on the other side of the world, then I would lose everything at home. All my programs. All my hopes to feed the hungry and shelter the homeless. All my dreams to provide education and medical care. . . . But if I left that war and let the communists take over . . . then I would be seen as a coward and my nation would be seen as an appeaser. . . . Oh, I could see it coming all right. . . . And Robert Kennedy would be right out in front leading the fight against me, telling everyone that I had betrayed John Kennedy's commitment to South Vietnam, . . . that I was a coward, an unmanly man.[10]

The American objective in Vietnam continued to be roughly as follows:

> We seek an independent non-Communist South Vietnam. We do not require that it serve as a Western base or as a member of a Western Alliance. South Vietnam must be free, however, to accept outside assistance. . . . Unless we can achieve this objective in South Vietnam, almost all of Southeast Asia will probably fall under Communist dominance and [pose] a "threat to" India, Australia, and Japan.

This was sometimes called the "domino theory."[11] Young people in the 1960s were becoming more vocal. In 1964, seventeen-year-olds became "the largest age

19

[group] in the U.S."[12] Businesses looked carefully at teen interests and buying habits. The new availability of FM radio and advertising response to "underground" publications caused record companies to spend large amounts of money supporting them. By the early 70s, rock music accounted for nearly 80 percent of all recorded music.[13]

Teens watched the Vietnam War carefully in part due to the fact that they and their siblings and friends were the ones going off to fight. At the war's peak, five hundred forty thousand Americans were in Vietnam. Yet young people had little power to decide our nation's degree of involvement. The Twenty-Sixth Amendment to the Constitution granting those eighteen and older the right to vote was not ratified until July 1, 1971.

Not all of the younger generation resisted the idea of our fighting in Vietnam; in fact, millions supported or ignored it. Many thousands gave their lives there. Best-selling music was not all acid rock and "protest songs"—it included soothing instrumentals and pro-war pieces too.[14]

High school and college students signed up for Reserve Officers Training Corps (ROTC), but others gave extra time to activities such as Red Cross, Chess Club, Future Homemakers of America, French Club, and athletics. It was a period when activist Stokely

This young military man is representative of the many teens who went off to war in Vietnam.

Carmichael was coining the term "black power."[15] It was also a time when a young man named Nolan Ryan was learning how to pitch a baseball after school.[16] Drug guru Timothy Leary was preaching a message of "Tune in, turn on, drop out."[17] But throngs of people in "the Jesus movement" were listening to the first "Christian music"—evangelistic lyrics set to guitars and drums.

Still other teens and young adults began to protest—not just the war but other matters. People protested against racism, the war, sexism, for legalization of drugs, communism, and "free love." On occasion, these different groups came together in their joint rejection of "the establishment" or "status quo."[18] A close look at three specific events will illustrate the methods and message of some of the more extreme campus protesters.

In 1968, certain students at such schools as Columbia University were unhappy with how the administration of the school handled complaints. They wanted changes, such as being allowed to hold indoor rallies and protests, having open hearings on disciplinary matters, and letting certain protesters who had already gotten in trouble go free.[19] Groups of the students moved into buildings, "raiding" classrooms and offices (sometimes vandalizing them and sometimes not). At San Francisco State, students drove a sound truck onto campus to make their message heard.[20] Campus Chancellor S. I. Hayakawa came out and pulled the wires to the speakers. He was "escorted back to his office by a bodyguard of . . . students."[21] Campuses soon "swarmed with reporters and television crews delighted with such colorful, outrageous events in their own backyard."[22] At Columbia, one building was "occupied" for so long that two students got married there. The bride wore a "heavy sweater, jeans, and white sneakers," and the groom was dressed in "maroon jeans, a white, high-collared Nehru jacket, beads, and black boots."[23] At San Francisco State, "the strikers [who refused to attend class] held daily noon rallies that routinely turned into raids."[24]

Eventually, at Columbia " . . . it seemed only police action could break the impasse . . . over a hundred students, faculty, and others were injured, though none critically. Over seven hundred people were arrested" there.[25]

Two student groups, Students for a Democratic Society (S.D.S) and the Student Nonviolent Coordinating Committee (S.N.C.C), were involved in another rally, at the Democratic National Convention in August of 1968. The convention was held in Chicago to let the party choose who their presidential candidate would be. Activist Jerry Rubin later said,

"We were not just innocent people who were victimized by the police. We came to plan a confrontation.[26] We're now in the business," he said, "of wholesale disruption and widespread resistance and dislocation of the American society."[27] Disruptions certainly occurred at the convention. Many were injured and many arrested, and neither hopeful candidate, Hubert Humphrey or George McCarthy, could probably have overcome the bad feelings the public had after seeing the violence on television. Instead, Richard Nixon won the election in November. He promised an "honorable end" to the Vietnam conflict and attacked the Great Society for "pouring billions of dollars into programs that have failed."[28]

Protests of the war and other issues were not always violent. The Tinkers were like thousands of others in wearing armbands, fasting, and doing other peaceful things to promote their causes. Dr. Martin Luther King, Jr., was famous for his nonviolent efforts to bring change. He is remembered for his efforts in the area of "civil disobedience." This sometimes meant peaceful but deliberate violation of the law in order to make a point, with the willingness to accept the legal consequences such as imprisonment. Like the Quakers, Dr. King stood for the concept that "Religious pacifism is . . . part of a larger Christian conviction and way of

Dr. Martin Luther King, Jr., was a pacifist. He was opposed to the Vietnam War, and all wars, as a violent means of settling disputes.

life."[29] His model was Jesus, who according to one scholar, "was more concerned that men should do justice than that they should get it."[30] From time to time, King would organize and participate in marches or sit-ins that might involve minor violations of the law such as "trespassing" upon whites-only property. Other such protesters were Daniel and Philip Berrigan, Catholics who felt that engaging in war was not consistent with their faith.

Protest of issues besides war and racism also gained attention. For example, feminism—organized activities on behalf of women's rights and interests—emerged in the 60s with "consciousness-raising" events, usually peaceful though sometimes shocking. In Washington, D.C., several feminist activists held a ritual "burial of traditional womanhood" during an anti-Vietnam demonstration.[31] In Atlantic City, outside the Miss America pageant, others threw such symbols of "feminine oppression" as underwear and dishwashing detergent into a trash can. At a bridal fair and show, some sang, "Here come the slaves/Off to their graves," and released 150 white mice.[32] These things were extreme, but they served to draw attention to real problems of inequities between men and women.

Also, the younger generation was not only concerned with protest. Most were characterized by new styles of dress, music, and expression. A press release written to promote a "Be-In" in California read: "Berkeley political activists and the love generation of the Haight-Ashbury will join together . . . to powwow, celebrate, and prophesy the epoch of liberation, love, peace, compassion, and unity of mankind."[33]

Jerry Rubin once said (or rather shouted), "The revolution is now. We create the revolution by living it."[34] For a few days at a popular concert called Woodstock, in August 1969, it seemed to be a revolution that could be lived. Overall, however, "The civil rights revolution has been easy to encourage and hard to live with," as one observer said in the 60s.[35]

Widespread changes were certainly taking place. Attitudes about authority as opposed to "autonomy," or personal freedom, were shifting. A magazine article titled "The Turned-on, Tuned-in World of Hippie Capitalists" said that "Nobody, but nobody, calls the boss by anything except his first name."[36] The courts were putting in place the desegregation ordered in the 1950s—opening public school classrooms to all races. The courts also took organized prayer out of the public schools. Landmark rulings on freedom of expression were being made. The Tinker case was decided by a Supreme Court that was, in itself, a topic of criticism by some. "We may forget that most Americans supported the war in Vietnam throughout the sixties, and that they opposed most of the specific objectives of both the civil rights and black power movements."[37] A Gallup poll in March 1968 showed that 63 percent of Americans considered the courts "too soft" on criminals. Another 1968 poll showed that 78 percent believed that "life today was getting worse in terms of morals."[38] It is true that X-rated theaters, pornography, and violence in films as well as on the street were all steadily increasing.[39] One Justice Department official said, "The values we held so dear are being shot. . . . Everything is being attacked—what you believed in and what you learned in school, in church, from your parents. So the middle class is sort of losing heart. They had their eyes on where they were going and suddenly it's all shifting sand."[40] A machinist said, "What I don't like about the students, the loud-mouthed ones, is that they think they know so much they can speak for everyone, because they're right and the rest of us aren't clever enough and can't talk like they can. . . ."[41]

Three particularly tragic events occurred in 1968, the last full year the *Tinker* case was being decided. (The decision was published in February of 1969.) One of the most memorable events was the assassination of Dr. Martin Luther King, Jr. An African-American soldier recalls an April day in Vietnam. He heard so much noise in the camp that he thought they were under attack. It was actually a reaction of those in the camp to the news that King was dead.[42] Within hours after King was shot, "racial violence erupted in 110 American cities."[43] African Americans were not only reacting to the murder. "The sixties' riots were riots of rising expectations. The people who took to the streets were men and women frustrated by the failure of America to deliver now on its promises of abundance and equality.... the effects of all these [Great Society] programs seemed at best marginal—and the ghettos could not wait."[44]

A second tragedy soon challenged the nation. Robert Kennedy, younger brother of the late president, was emerging as a possible alternative to Lyndon Johnson as the Democrats' presidential nominee in November's election. He had actively helped his brother run for office, and later said, "... I had time to watch everything—I filled complete notebooks with notes on how a Presidential campaign should be run."[45] But Robert Kennedy too was shot by an assassin, Sirhan Sirhan.

Another blow to the nation was the "Tet offensive." This was an attack on the South Vietnamese by the North Vietnamese during a Buddhist holiday called Tet on January 30. It was "the most concentrated and ferocious campaign since the end of WWII. . . ."[46] The losses to American and South Vietnamese lives caused an "earthquake in mainstream public opinion," and were "a critical ingredient in the retreat from Vietnam."[47] Lyndon Johnson assembled some cabinet officers and advisers such as Supreme Court Justice Abe Fortas. There was a meeting in March about how to get North Vietnam to the bargaining table.[48] It seemed that around that time a turning point was reached, and Johnson made up his mind. Due to health concerns and fear of voter rejection, he decided that his next major speech would announce a bombing halt. He would also use the speech as the occasion to withdraw from the 1968 race. Coupling the two would convince the Communists that his proposal was "a serious and sincere effort to find a road to peace."[49] Talks with North Vietnam began in Paris on May 10. The next President, Richard Nixon, began the "Vietnamization" of the war, handing back the fighting to the South Vietnamese.[50] A treaty was finally signed in 1973 ending United States involvement in Vietnam.

Perhaps without the protests of people like Mary Beth Tinker, more lives would have been lost. One scholar said that the peace movement "made a difference on the conduct of the war."[51] Years later, another young woman, a college student born in the Midwest,

Thousands of people visit the Vietnam Veterans Memorial each year to honor the memory of friends and loved ones lost in the Vietnam War.

made a difference. Architect and artist Maya Lin's design was selected as the winning entry from almost fifteen hundred ideas for the Vietnam Veterans Memorial in Washington, D.C. Now thousands of people each year visit the Memorial's black wall engraved with the names of the dead, to remember and honor, and say, "Here is the price we paid."[52]

3

From Classroom to Courtroom

When school was back in session in January 1966, the students returned without armbands. But the matter was not settled. Eventually their parents hired attorneys to litigate the matter (try it in court). The school district's attorneys were ready to defend.

The lawsuit asked for two primary things—one was an injunction, an order from the court to stop the school district from enforcing its rule against black armbands and interfering with free speech. The other thing requested was "nominal" damages. This means that only a very small amount of money was sought for the violation of the plaintiffs' civil rights—in this case, one dollar. If the students had been beaten or had property taken from them, they could have asked for "actual" damages. They also asked for the costs associated with bringing the case to court. To take even a factually simple case, which this one was, from the initial stage all the way to the Supreme Court can cost tens of thousands of dollars. Anyone suing has to realize that he or she is also costing the opponent about the same amount of time and money to defend against the suit. People only have a right to free legal help if they are too poor to defend themselves against accusation of a crime. This was not the case here. As plaintiffs bringing a lawsuit, the Tinkers were on the offensive, not the defensive. The American Civil Liberties Union however, was assisting them to pay the costs.

They sued under a law, or statute, that had been passed long ago to enforce the Bill of Rights guaranteed in our Constitution. That law was Section 1 of the Civil Rights Act of 1871.[1] When the Civil War ended, former slaves had to find a place in society.

Many whites, especially in the South, did not change their racist attitudes overnight. They did not try to cooperate with the new laws protecting blacks. In fact, some of the worst offenders were city and county officials such as law enforcement officers who did nothing if they saw crimes being committed against African

Americans.[2] So the federal government made it an offense to deprive people of their civil rights "under color of law," that is, using the "cloak of authority" to do wrong or allow it to be done.[3] By the time Mary Beth Tinker was in school, the law had expanded to make even school boards liable if they stood in the way of people's federally-protected rights. In her case, for example, every member of the school board was sued, along with others, all called defendants.

The plaintiffs, or persons bringing the complaint into Federal District court, were John and Mary Beth Tinker, Christopher Eckhardt, and their fathers. A "minor," or someone under age eighteen, can not normally sue alone, since any agreement the young person might make during the litigation is unenforceable. The Tinkers hired Dan Johnston, a dedicated lawyer from the area. He would eventually be assisted by others. The defendants' attorney was someone who had worked with the school district on a variety of legal needs for quite a while. However, when this case arose, not everyone in the law firm agreed with the approach the school district had taken. Only those who were supportive of it went ahead.[4] The "lead counsel" in the case, who eventually argued before the Supreme Court, was Allen Herrick, affectionately known as "Judge" because he had served as a local judge thirty years before.[5]

The trial took place in July. It was "tried to the bench"—there was no jury, only a judge. The witnesses for the plaintiffs took the stand until 3:25 P.M.; the defense only took fifteen more minutes.[6] The school took the approach earlier taken in a case called *Gobitis* v. *Minersville School District*.[7] There, the Supreme Court upheld a school requirement that every child salute the flag. The Court said the state had an important interest in developing patriotism in youngsters, even if a student claimed his or her conscience would not permit saluting. But that case was no longer the law, and "the weight of authority," case law, appeared to be on the side of the Tinkers.

The most current and applicable cases were a pair of decisions, handed down together in 1966 by the Fifth Circuit Court of Appeals, the federal court appeal level just under the Supreme Court. Since the Tinkers lived in the Eighth Circuit, their judge did not have to follow the rulings, but he could consider them. The first was *Burnside* v. *Byars*, which presented the following facts:[8]

Some African-American students at a public school in the South wore "freedom buttons" which carried logos suggesting racial unity and the letters S.N.C.C., standing for Student Nonviolent Coordinating

Committee, a controversial activist organization. The students were told not to wear the buttons the next day. Thirty to forty students did. The principal suspended them for a week. Some parents sued to prevent enforcement of the rule against the buttons. Two years later, the Fifth Circuit declared that since the record showed "no interference with educational activity," the buttons should have been allowed.[9]

> Wearing buttons . . . is certainly not in the class of those activities which inherently distract students and break down the regimen of the classroom such as carrying banners, scattering leaflets, and speechmaking, all of which are protected methods of expression, but all of which have no place in an orderly classroom.[10]

Often when a court issues two opinions the same day, it is not coincidence; the two are meant to be read together and balance each other. The "companion case" to *Burnside* was *Blackwell* v. *Issaquena County Board of Education*.[11] The facts were almost identical, but here, some button wearers "were creating a disturbance by noisily talking in the hall when they were scheduled to be in class."[12] Moreover, some bothered others and pinned buttons on them even when the buttons were not wanted. One wearer who had been sent home entered a class and told another student to leave. Once out of the building, some suspended students threw buttons in through the open windows.

"There was an unusual degree of commotion, boisterous conduct, a collision with the rights of others, an undermining of school authority. . . ."[13] The Court did not have much trouble concluding that here, the students had abused their rights.

The Tinkers could only hope that their actions would be viewed as more like those in *Burnside* than in *Blackwell.* But some people were not convinced. John Tinker's principal had testified:

> I reminded John that we had a short time previously had a school program in observance of Veteran's Day, at which time I personally had appeared before the student body expressing my concern with respect to the war dead . . . that there were appropriate times for us to mourn our war dead, . . . and it did not seem appropriate or necessary to me to mourn them as he was doing at this time.[14]

Another witness testified that if Mary Beth Tinker "didn't like the way our elected officials were handling things," the proper response was through "the ballot box and not in the halls of our public schools." Of course, it was actually impossible for any thirteen-year-old to vote at the ballot box.[15] Vice Principal Donald Blackman said:

> I suppose I recall students wearing religious symbols such as crosses and things of that sort to Roosevelt [Chris Eckhardt's school] from time to time. I suppose there would be political buttons involving

campaigns for president and vice president; I never really noticed, frankly. There is no regulation against this sort of political demonstration.[16]

John Tinker admitted, "I suppose I was attracting some attention by wearing the armband."[17] Yet no one had any evidence of a real disruption resulting from the armbands. The next day the lawyers returned and made their closing arguments. Then the trial was over.

About five weeks later the judge returned his order: "Plaintiffs' request for injunction and nominal damages, is denied, at plaintiffs' costs." The Federal District Court acknowleged that the facts were essentially the same as in *Burnside*, but it accurately observed that it was not bound to come to the same conclusion as another circuit's court.[18] While the court recognized the armbands as symbolic speech covered by the First Amendment, it held that the school policy was a reasonable effort to prevent disturbance.[19]

Now the Tinkers could quit, or they could appeal the decision. They appealed to the next higher court—the Eighth Circuit. They sent "the record," the evidence produced in the trial court, and wrote briefs—legal arguments—challenging the result from the lower court. They could not offer additional evidence. They could only show that somehow the court had incorrectly applied the law or had drawn

Thousands of men and women died in Vietnam while the *Tinker* case was making its way through the courts.

unreasonable conclusions from the facts. The District Court had found that *Tinker* was different from *Burnside* because the war issue was now so surrounded by emotion and violence that the Des Moines school system could be a little stricter about speech than otherwise would have been permissible. This, according to the Tinkers, was an error of judicial reasoning called considering facts outside the record—in other words, the judge was using facts or feelings about Des Moines not presented as evidence, to make his decision.[20] They also complained that other symbols, such as campaign buttons, were allowed, but not this particular form of speech. The defendants, after reading the plaintiffs' brief, then responded with a written brief, emphasizing that the school had to avoid disruption and that the protesters could find other means of opposing the war. Then both went to oral arguments. This is similar to a debate, but the judges can interrupt to ask questions. Three judges heard the case, and both sides probably thought they were finished. But the Eighth Circuit notified them they were wanted again to argue before the full panel of judges—*en banc.* This was a close case, and the Eighth Circuit was not deciding hastily.

Back in Des Moines, the community reacted to the acts of the students. "People threw red paint at our house,

41

and we got lots of calls," Mary Tinker has since related. "We got all kinds of threats to our family. . . . People called our house on Christmas Eve and said the house would be blown up by morning."[21]

When the Eighth Circuit ruled, again the Tinkers had lost. The court was evenly divided and issued no opinion. The court simply let stand the lower court's ruling that "the reactions and comments of other students as a result of the armbands would be likely to disturb the disciplined atmosphere required for any classroom."[22] It was November 3, 1967—almost two years after the students' decision to wear their armbands.

It was time to evaluate the chances of success in the Supreme Court. Each side turned to their lawyers. The American Civil Liberties Union was assisting the Tinkers and Eckhardts, primarily to lend a hand on the brief, or written arguments, and to add the expertise of their attorney, Melvin L. Wulf. He was National Legal Director for the A.C.L.U. at the time, and the final decision to take the case had been his. "We had a receptive court," he says, "and I knew it was a strong case."[23] He worked hard with Dan Johnston, crossing the miles between them with long distance phone calls and lots of special delivery mail. Wulf finally met Dan Johnston and thought he embodied the Midwest—"He was rather tall, and light-haired—he looked like a sheaf of wheat," Wulf recalls.

The Supreme Court looked as though it would probably favor the the petitioners (the Tinkers). However, most people watching the Court, including the respondents' attorney Allan H. Herrick, were aware that Chief Justice Earl Warren might be stepping down. Who would take his place? If a "law-and-order" Chief Justice took over, would he have time to sway the Court in favor of the schools' position before the case was voted on? "If this goes to a Warren Court, we will not win the day," he predicted to his daughter.[24] Counsel for the other side could be no more confident. During the term for which the case was set for argument, 1968, more campus protests broke out.

> Autumn 1968 was a tumultuous period for the student[s]. . . . The new semester was scarcely under way when violence swept the nation's campuses. . . . Radical students at the University of Washington in Seattle that fall danced by the light of a burning R.O.T.C. building to the chant:
> This is number one
> And the fun has just begun,
> Burn it down, burn it down, burn it down.[25]

At oral arguments before the Supreme Court, the defense attempted to draw a connection between the plaintiffs and Students for a Democratic Society.[26] Some members of the group had since evolved into the

Weathermen, an even more radical group, which resorted to bombings and bank robberies to make their point.[27] This was just the type of publicity the Tinkers' cause did not need.

On the other hand, on December 1, 1968, the nation watched the Selective Service drawing numbers for the first draft lottery. Men were placed in line for military service according to the order in which their birthday was drawn. Nixon had been elected president on the promise of peace in Vietnam.[28] Perhaps the Justices would be sympathetic too with the Tinkers' demand for peace.

A case almost always comes before the Supreme Court by *writ of certiorari.* The Justices must vote to decide whether they want to hear the case at all, or "grant cert." Four votes are required to grant certiorari. Sometimes they leave undisturbed an opinion they do not agree with, but usually they grant cert on important issues. Abe Fortas did not want to hear the case. He questioned whether the Constitution "authorizes us to intervene in school discipline matters except where discrimination or clear abuse is involved."[29] But he later wrote a comment on a memo that said, "this is a tough case & probably will be granted."[30] By a vote of five to four, it was.

A new voice was also soon heard on the matter—the

It was during the transition from the Johnson administration to that of Nixon that the *Tinker* case was decided.

United States National Student Association filed a brief called an *amicus curiae*, or "friend of the court" brief. If the Court permits it, someone outside the case can make arguments to the Court. Here, the student association supported the Tinkers. It particularly attacked the school's policy as a "prior restraint." This is a limit on speech before the speech occurs.[31] Moreover, it said, the controlling law was *West Virginia State Board of Education* v. *Barnette*.[32] In that situation, some children who were Jehovah's Witnesses were enrolled in public school and refused to participate in a salute to the flag. The Supreme Court had seen the flag salute as a political statement that could indeed violate the children's beliefs. The Court struck down "the brutal compulsion that requires a sensitive and conscientious child to stultify himself [silence his conscience] in public."[33] This was a case on which the petitioners (plaintiffs in the court below; the defendants were now respondents—responding to the petition) also relied.[34] In the next chapter, we shall see how Justice Fortas applied these precedents, as well as those that follow.

The Tinkers' attorneys had to deal with at least two recent cases: *United States* v. *O'Brien*, which was decided on May 28, 1968, and *Adderley* v. *Florida*, which had been on the books for two years.[35] In both cases, conduct rather than speech had caused a problem. In both, the protesters had lost. The petitioners limited these cases to the purpose of the law, to forbid the conduct—and not to clamp down on communication. For example, in *Adderley*, protesting college students were arrested for trespassing. The trespass law had not been directed at them and their speech. But the armbands had been explicitly forbidden, and were only worn to communicate a message.[36]

The petitioners had to emphasize high ideals to be persuasive. They repeatedly warned that schools not only teach their subject matter, but also teach attitudes, and that the school must teach by example that peaceful free expression is tolerated.

> [T]he principle of free speech, as embodied in the First Amendment, will not be recognized by our citizens as fundamental to our society unless that principle is a living reality during their formative school years. . . . [These principles] which are to be encouraged in the adult democratic society must affirmatively be fostered in the school system. . . . The classroom is peculiarly the market-place of ideas. The Nation's future depends upon leaders trained through wide exposure of ideas which discovers truth out of a multitude of tongues, [rather] than through any kind of authoritative selection.[37]

The respondent school also had some distinctions to make and some dire warnings if the Court ruled against it. It leaned as hard on *Blackwell* as the petitioners had on *Burnside*. The rule against armbands was a "reasonable rule necessary for the maintenance of school discipline."[38] Herrick dug up the evidence so crucial to proving his point in the record: "At the meeting in his father's office [December 19, 1965] John attended and there were accounts of physical violence over wearing armbands. Either Bruce Clark or Ross [Peterson, friends of John's] said somebody had struck John. Except for the prompt action by the school administration, the problem might well have developed into the type of demonstration that has been witnessed throughout the country in the past two or three years."[39]

Apparently the incident Herrick found had taken place off campus, because there was nothing else in the record he could point to in terms of physical conflict. The way the statement was recounted in the record, it should probably be considered merely hearsay—unreliable evidence from sources outside the lawsuit. Would it be sufficient proof to convince the Supreme Court of the risks the school district faced? Or would Chris Eckhardt and the Tinkers win after all?

4

Abe Fortas and the Warren Court

Abe Fortas wrote the opinion that we refer to today as *Tinker* v. *Des Moines.* He joined a Court that was possibly the most controversial and influential in history. He referred to that era of the Supreme Court's work as "the most profound and pervasive revolution ever achieved by substantially peaceful means."[1] The leadership of its Chief Justice, Earl Warren, was a major reason for that, but other factors existed as well. The first African-American Justice, Thurgood Marshall, was appointed in 1967 and brought new perspectives to the Court. The sweeping *Brown* v. *Board of Education* decision, although it was handed down over ten years before, remained on people's minds. It still had to be

49

implemented to desegregate schools, district by district, all over the land. Abe Fortas himself caused the Court to be caught up in conflict the likes of which the Court had not seen in its history.

Justice Fortas was born to Orthodox Jewish parents in Tennessee. Not only was he a bright student growing up, but he played in a jazz band and worked in stores to earn extra money. After teaching law for a time at Yale, he became a successful corporate attorney. He also took an interest in those who had no voice in society. For example, he agreed to take to the Supreme Court the case of Clarence Earl Gideon. Gideon was a penniless Florida inmate who had tried to act as his own attorney in defending himself against criminal charges. Through Fortas's work for his client, a new case law established the right of everyone accused of a serious crime to have the assistance of an attorney.[2] Fortas also worked to expand the rights of young people, especially when they faced conflict with authorities.[3] For these reasons, one would expect him to rule in favor of the Tinkers. But for him, there could also be powerful reasons not to.

One of Fortas's closest friends was Lyndon Johnson. In fact, President Johnson (LBJ) had offered Fortas a seat on the Supreme Court and Fortas declined. But

Abe Fortas (left) was named to his post on the Supreme Court by President Johnson (right). Johnson and Fortas were friends.

Johnson did not like to take "no" for an answer. One historian describes what happened next:

> "Come on over and attend today's press conference," coaxed Lyndon Johnson over the telephone. "I'm going to be making a statement on Vietnam." Sitting in the workroom of his firm's red brick Victorian mansion, Abe Fortas dutifully put aside a brief he planned to submit to the Supreme Court in the fall. As it turned out, LBJ had more in mind than Vietnam troop movements. By the time the news conference ended, the case lawyer Fortas hoped to take to the Court was forgotten. He was going there himself.[4]

The announcement of the president's choice for the next Justice was so sudden that Mrs. Fortas learned of it while watching television.

Many people felt that Fortas and Johnson were too close as friends to work together. They noted that an idea called "separation of powers" requires that the three branches of our government remain independent of each other. Fortas, a member of the judicial branch, and LBJ, the chief of the executive branch, conferred frequently. Sometimes the president invited the Justice to the highest-level decision-making and advisory meetings. "There were times when [the president] called me when he needed my counsel, I admit that," Fortas later commented.[5] So in regard to the *Tinker* case, Fortas faced a challenge. LBJ was carrying on the war, and Fortas himself supported it.[6] How could he write a decision that allowed high school students to protest that war? Who could predict what might flow from the liberty he would give if he ruled in favor of antiwar protest? Could he walk the fine line in his opinion between allowing protest and allowing chaos? How he answered these questions will be addressed later. But the other eight Justices each had a vote—how would they rule?

The Chief Justice during the *Tinker* deliberations was Earl Warren. Young Earl grew up in Bakersfield, California, a "dusty frontier railroad town" complete with saloons, gambling joints, and cockfights.[7] One of his first jobs was to seek out the railroad crew, sometimes found in the seediest areas of town, to tell them their shift was coming up. Another was to help deliver blocks of ice—there was no refrigeration at the time. Then he delivered for a bakery. "There wasn't any of the precious ice to take home," he recalls, "but there were plenty of cookies."[8] As he roamed the town, he had contact with Hispanic and Italian families, French sheepmen, Chinese railway builders, bandits, and lawmen. He saw much of life, and seemed to see it with compassion.[9]

Warren may have had experiences as a youth that made him more inclined to rule in favor of the Tinkers. He remembers being "too small and immature to be

President Johson meets with leaders of the nations assisting in the Vietnam War in October 1966.

taken seriously" and writes of the times he was paddled at school by the principal when he was an eighth grader (the same grade Mary Beth Tinker was in) and as a senior unfairly expelled from school, an act that the County Board of Education reversed the same day.[10]

He served in the Army, then as a District Attorney boldly prosecuting crimes, and later as governor of California. When appointed to the Supreme Court, he tackled the job with characteristic gusto. He later said:

> My years on the Court were crowded with cases involving segregation, voting rights, and . . . incursions on the Bill of Rights . . . —all of which had an emotional impact on large segments of the nation. Such cases would provoke controversy regardless of the way they might be decided. I, of course, understood that . . . no judge can satisfy both sides, particularly in emotion-charged cases. Therefore, I never took personally objection to the criticism leveled at me or the Court, and made no attempt to justify publicly any of our decisions.[11]

Disagreement was present inside as well as outside the walls of the Supreme Court. Through the years, Warren had done a fine job of bringing the Justices to unity, but he usually faced a challenge when it came to some of the more opinionated members of the Court.[12] On free speech, they all had opinions.

William J. Brennan, Jr., was part of what one scholar called "the liberal-activist" element of the Court, an element that Warren led. That meant they were willing to make changes in society through the court system in a special effort to benefit less-privileged people. He was a consistent defender of free speech. But Brennan also had "the judge's strong sense of precedent," meaning that he believed that earlier Court rulings must control his rulings even if he did not fully approve of them.[13] He was a Catholic, a father of four, and a good-natured man. It was he who, when Abe Fortas appeared years later before the Court as an attorney again, welcomed him back with a broad smile.[14]

William O. Douglas, an avid sportsman and father of two, was at the time one of the older members of the Court. He is remembered as an eloquent supporter of liberty. One commentator says that to him, "the essence of the Constitution is freedom—as much as possible—for the individual." He was "seldom content with the Court's position, even its most liberal stands."[15] He could be expected to support Mary Beth Tinker.

Thurgood Marshall was most likely another vote for Tinker. He was a staunch liberal who had learned to practice law fighting for the National Association for the Advancement of Colored People (N.A.A.C.P.). He wrote strong opinions favoring parties accused of obscenity and protected the rights of picketers. He is also remembered as an attorney litigating before the Supreme Court, when he successfully argued for desegregating the public schools in *Brown* v. *Board of Education*.[16]

Byron White was a former football player for what is now the Pittsburgh Steelers, and was at one time the leading ground gainer in the NFL. He had never been a judge before when he was appointed to the Supreme Court.[17] Once on the bench, he could see the value of limiting free speech in some cases where law and order could be jeopardized, and he felt that the more activist of his fellow Justices must think that ". . . the Constitution is an empty vessel into which judges may pour any social policy they see fit."[18] Sometimes he was aggressive, even abrupt, in his manner of discussing cases. But he was a practical and level-headed judge.[19]

Potter Stewart, former reporter, Naval officer, and lawyer, had a more moderate view than some of his "Brethren," as the Justices on the Court were traditionally called. "During the heyday of the Warren Court, he was more often than not found on the cautious, conservative side. . . ."[20] But to the *Tinker* case, he brought his "generous approach" to freedom of speech and the press. Perhaps it came from his days as a reporter. In any case, he had the "independence of mind" that made him hard to predict on this case.[21] It was he who said of hard-core pornography, "I know it when I see it."[22] The bluntness of the phrase was typical of him— he has proved to be one of the most quotable of the Justices, crafting his decisions with just the right words and trying, unlike many of his colleagues, to write the narrowest ruling possible.

Justice Harlan was a wealthy and brilliant man, "a product of Princeton and Oxford, polished by his experiences in a Wall Street firm."[23] He "did not share the activist views of the Warren Court majority in the 1960's" and was more inclined to restrict free speech if he saw harm to others coming from it.[24]

Yet, while Justice Fortas was writing the opinion in *Tinker*, Harlan was carefully writing in his own hand the opinion in *Street* v. *New York*. This said that a state could not outlaw disrespectful treatment of the American flag. Harlan based this ruling squarely on First Amendment freedom, and four Justices, including Fortas, dissented (recorded their disagreement) to that opinion.[25] Unlike Justice Fortas, who was very active off the bench and involved with the president, Justice Harlan felt a Supreme Court Justice should completely remove himself from politics and personal interests, to the point of not even voting in presidential elections. He was a gentle and considerate man, and may have been the only man on the Court with a known handicap—he was functionally blind in his last six years on the bench, during which he heard this case.[26]

Finally, there was Justice Hugo Black. He had been on the Court long before Justice Fortas, and he had been known for a position of "First Amendment absolutism." In other words:

> As Black intoned again and again, the First Amendment command that "Congress shall make no law . . . abridging the freedom of speech or of the press" means precisely that. . . . To proffered demurrer, usually beginning, "But, Mr. Justice," Black's instant if gentle response would be, "But, nothing." Lifting the ten-cent copy of his beloved Constitution from his pocket, he would ask his questioner to read the words of the First Amendment. When the latter would reach the phrase, "no law," Black would utter a soft "thank you."[27]

Yet lately, Black had been uttering his own "but's" to his absolute rule, and he had lately been at odds with Fortas on significant issues. One historian says he had "become crotchety in his eighties."[28]

It was these nine men who gathered to hear oral arguments in the *Tinker* case on November 12, 1968. Richard Nixon had just been elected president, Fortas was under fire for alleged misconduct, and Chief Justice Warren was near to ending his career. But all these things were put aside as people gathered in the room—draped in red, lined with marble columns, and supplied with quill pens—in which arguments were to be heard. Dan Johnston, as attorney for the petitioners, argued first.

Under Court rules he had a limited time allotted and he would be signalled by a light when it was time to halt, even if he was in the middle of a sentence. He could be interrupted at any time by one of the Justices, though never by the other side. He spoke evenly but forcefully, in a reporter's voice. "Mr. Chief Justice, and may it please the Court. The conduct of the students essentially was this. That at Christmastime in 1965, they decided that they should wear small black arm-bands to express certain views which they had in regard to the war in Vietnam." He described their views and what happened when they wore the armbands to class. Justice Byron White spoke up.

> **White:** What if the student had gotten up from the class he went to and delivered the message orally that his armband was intended to convey and insisted on doing it all through the hour?
>
> **Johnston:** In that case, Your Honor, we would not be here, even if he insisted on doing it only for a second, because he would clearly be—although he would be expressing his views, he would be doing something else.
>
> **White:** Why did they wear the armband to class, to express that message?
>
> **Johnston:** To express that message, yes.

White: To everybody in the class?

Johnston: To everyone in the class, yes, Your Honor.

[The Justice's voice, at first musing and muted, began to take on more of an edge.]

White: Everybody while they were listening to some other subject matter was supposed to be looking at the armband and taking in that message?

Johnston: Well, to the extent that they would see it. . . . They were intended to see it in a way that would not be distracting . . .

White: And to understand it.

Johnston: And to understand it.

White: And to absorb that message . . .

Johnston: And to absorb the message . . .

White: While they're studying arithmetic . . . they're supposed to be taking in this message about Vietnam?

Johnston: Well, except that, Your Honor, I believe that the method that the students chose in this particular instance was specifically designed in such a way that it would not cause that kind of disruption.

White: . . . They anticipated students would see it and understand it and think about it?

Johnston: That's correct.

White: And when they did it in class, they intended the students to do it in class?

Johnston: I think they intended, I think they chose a message, chose a method of expression, Your Honor, which would not be distracting . . .

White: . . . [P]hysically; it wouldn't make a noise, it wouldn't cause a commotion, but don't you think it would cause some people to direct their attention to the armband and the Vietnam War and think about that, rather than what they were thinking about, supposed to be thinking about in the classroom?

Johnston: I think perhaps, Your Honor, it might for a few moments have done that, and I think it perhaps might have distracted some students, just as many other things do in the classroom which are allowed, from time to time.[29]

The attorney then explained that freedom of expression under the First Amendment was at stake. He was questioned about other forms of speech—campaign buttons and placards. Fortas said, "Suppose some child shows up in school wearing an outlandish costume . . . and this child says I am wearing this outlandish costume because I want to express the very strong belief I have in the utmost freedom of the individual."[30] But Johnston avoided the temptation of bogging down in finer and finer distinctions between types of speech and simply reminded the Justices that no real disruption was shown in the evidence. That kept the case squarely in the ideal position for the Court's attention, since they were not being asked to go back and decide whether amounts of evidence proved this or that. When a case is appealed, the higher court is basically "stuck" with the record from the original trial. The

Supreme Court's jurisdiction is instead usually limited to determining whether the Constitution was violated or not. Thus Johnston soon concluded, "[W]e'd like to have the same principles applied in the school . . . that are applied elsewhere."[31]

Next Allan Herrick stood up to argue for the school board, the respondents. (The students were the petitioners.) His tone was more conversational. "Now, in substance, if we understand the petitioners' position in this case, it is that the school officials are powerless to act until the disruption occurs. Respondents believe that should not be the rule. Sometimes an ounce of prevention is a lot better than a pound of cure, and I think the subsequent history of such activities bear out the judgment of the school officials. . . ." Herrick may have been referring to the many injuries, arrests, and destruction of property that had taken place on college campuses during the year. But Justice Marshall was not impressed:

> **Herrick:** [Reading from a statement] "A former student at one of our high schools was killed in Vietnam. Some of his friends are still in school. It was felt that if any kind of demonstration existed, it might evolve into something which would be difficult to control."

> **Marshall:** Do we have a city in this country that hasn't had someone killed in Vietnam?

Herrick: No, I think not, Your Honor, but I don't think it would be an explosive situation in most cases. But if someone is going to appear in court with an armband here, protesting the thing, that could be explosive. . . .

Marshall: It could be.

Herrick: What?

Marshall: It could be. Is that your position? And there is no evidence that it would be? Is that the rule you want us to adopt?

Herrick: No, not at all, Your Honor.

The attorney offered several phrases for the Justices to employ as tests when he summarized: ". . . [T]his Court must determine how far it wants to go under the Constitutional amendments for free speech in reviewing every decision of every school district made in good faith, in its reasonable discretion and judgment, as necessary to maintain order and a scholarly, disciplined atmosphere within the classroom."[32]

Arguments concluded, the next step was for the Justices to discuss the case at conference. As they gathered three days later to do so, they no doubt observed the traditional way of beginning the meeting: each Justice shook hands with the eight others, to remind them that "despite their differences, all members of the Court shared a unity of purpose."[33] How different this

This portrait of the members of the Supreme Court was taken in 1967. The Justices shown are as follows: Front row from left to right: John Marshall Harlan, Hugo Black, Earl Warren, William Douglas, and William J. Brennan, Jr. Back row from left to right: Abe Fortas, Potter Stewart, Byron White, and Thurgood Marshall.

was from the violent responses that some outside the Court were giving to those who disagreed with them. Then the Justices began to talk. No one else was allowed in the room. Younger Justices spoke first, to avoid being influenced by their senior colleagues. Strict secrecy of these discussions is maintained so that those involved can speak freely, and change their minds without embarrassment.[34]

Justices Black and Harlan were for affirming, or upholding, the lower courts. But Fortas said, in his soft-spoken way, that schools "must show some shred of justification in the sense of a prohibition necessary to carrying on school functions. But here no justification was shown."[35] Fortas's statement there gives a clue to how he would eventually write the opinion. He was putting the "burden of proof" on the school to show it was right, not on the students to show it was wrong. This might seem a small difference, but in fact, the question of who bears the burden of proof is often the decisive question in a case. If each side presents equally weighty facts and arguments, then the one who had the burden of proof loses. And that indeed would be the result in *Tinker*.

But other Justices had input, too. Warren wanted to reverse the lower courts and favor the students, but his approach was based on the unfairness that only certain kinds of symbols were forbidden. That, he was sure, violated the principle of equal protection of the laws. The "bottom line" to Earl Warren was always, "Is it fair?" and he was always striving for a result to which he could answer "yes."[36] Byron White, described as the "Greek ideal of a sound mind in a sound body," reasoned, "If the authorities are empowered to maintain order, they must be able to classify what disrupts communication among students. . . . But the state doesn't defend this on that ground, but on a physically disruptive ground of which there's no evidence."[37]

After the conference, the Justice appointed to write the majority opinion would begin his draft and then circulate it to the others for comment before publishing it. Justice Fortas was assigned that task. It would be one of the last opinions he ever wrote. Meanwhile, Justice Black settled down to write one of the most scorching dissents of all time.

5

The Decision

In writing a judicial opinion, a Justice must review the cases and statutes that both sides have cited, as well as all others which may influence the decision.

Justice Fortas was not one to quote many cases in his opinions, but he did master them before setting forth his views. Some of the cases most applicable to *Tinker* will be summarized here.

In the early fall of 1968, just six months before *Tinker*, Chief Justice Earl Warren had written an opinion in *United States* v. *O'Brien*. Justice Fortas had joined in that opinion. Knowing that he was violating federal law, David O'Brien had burned his Selective Service registration certificate on the steps of the South Boston Courthouse in front of "a sizable crowd."[1] He said he did it "publicly to influence others to adopt his antiwar beliefs."[2] Warren did not focus on the speech aspect of O'Brien's actions, but rather on the law itself, which had been passed long before, against destroying the certificates, or draft cards. Warren said that when conduct is outlawed for a legitimate reason, then the illegal conduct will not be excused even if it was done to express an idea.[3] But the case was not related to the school environment. Would that make a difference? Because Warren had assigned the drafting of the *Tinker* decision to Abe Fortas, Warren would be letting Fortas answer that question.

In *Gobitis* v. *Minersville School District*, a 1940 case, a twelve-year-old girl, Lillian Gobitis, and her ten-year-old brother, William, were expelled from their public school for refusing to salute the American flag. The Supreme Court was asked to overturn the expulsion, but it declined to do so. To review the school board's actions would "in effect make us the school board for the country," said Justice Felix Frankfurter, who was no longer on the bench when Fortas was serving.[4] The school in the *Gobitis* case had argued that compelling every child to salute the flag was worthwhile training in patriotism, but the children said it violated their consciences. The Court sided with the school and decided that "help[ing] toward a common feeling for the common country" was a legitimate goal.[5]

In 1969, Ken Love burned both his draft card and his S.D.S. membership card "to show [his] deepest digust for the violent ways of both S.D.S. and the U.S.A."

Besides, to allow some to be exempt from the ceremony "might cast doubts in the minds of the other children."[6] The case had been decided in 1940—with war on the horizon. Was it not also necessary to protect youngsters in 1968 from disturbing and unpatriotic views when the nation was so conflicted and violent? That had been the rationale for the Des Moines schools' policy.

The Court raised an additional interesting point: if Minersville parents were unhappy with the school's policy, they could vote on it and make changes. "To fight out the wise use of legislative authority in the forum of public opinion" rather than in the "judicial arena, serves to vindicate the self-confidence of a free people."[7] Passing the hot potato from the Court to the legislature has long been a favorite technique when the judiciary does not want to get involved—but it was out of keeping with the activist, hands-on approach of the Court of which Fortas was a part.

Only three years after *Gobitis*, in 1943, the Court was presented with almost identical facts in *West Virginia State Board of Education* v. *Barnette*. The students there could not salute the flag because they could not "bow down" to a "graven image" according to the passage in the Old Testament teaching the Ten Commandments—Exodus 20: 4-5. But this time the

Court analyzed the dilemma of the students not as a religious one but as a matter of free speech. Noting that the students' behavior was "peaceful and orderly," as was the Tinkers', the Court said that making the students salute the flag was actually forcing them to make a symbolic statement or else surrender their chance at public education, punishing both child and parent.[8] The Court now looked upon the flag as the state's symbol. Symbolism, the opinion said, is "a short cut from mind to mind."[9]

What about letting the legislative branch of the government handle the question? In just three years, the Court had changed its position. "The very purpose of the Bill of Rights was to withdraw certain subjects from the vicissitudes [changes] of political controversy. . . . One's right to life, liberty, and property, to free speech, a free press, freedom of worship and assembly, and other fundamental rights may not be submitted to vote; they depend on the outcome of no elections."[10] That approach fit with the obvious view of the Court that in *Tinker*, the Court system should get involved. Otherwise they could have just voted to "deny cert," and let the lower court ruling stand. The *Barnette* Court then overruled *Gobitis* and held that the school had acted unconstitutionally.

Was this the decisive case on the *Tinker* facts as

well? Not really—in *Tinker*, the students were not being coerced (forced) to make a statement they did not believe. No one suggested that taking off the armbands was the same as being forced to say the Vietnam War was a good thing. But *Barnette* was a fine example of the weighing of free speech and school authority. Free speech was the resounding winner.

Yet free expression is not a magic charm for winning school cases. Justice Fortas took careful note of circumstances where students had merely violated a dress code and called upon the First Amendment for their defense.[11]

For example, in *Ferrell* v. *Dallas Independent School District,* a 1968 case, three boys in a rock band were denied enrollment at their public high school "because of their 'Beatle' type haircuts."[12] The manager or booking agent for the band was quite vocal about the boys' indignation over the school policy on hair length, and called the media to complain that their civil rights had been violated under both the Texas and federal Constitutions. The band even recorded a song in protest, which the local stations played for a few days.[13] There was testimony that occasional fistfights and foul language cropped up over "long hair," though other witnesses said that long hair was well accepted in the schools in Dallas.[14] The ruling? That school districts can adopt such rules and regulations, including hair and dress codes, as they deem proper to govern and manage their schools.[15]

This case was not difficult to distinguish from *Tinker*. The boys with Beatle hairstyles merely wanted the freedom to dress as they chose. This was not, Fortas reasoned, "symbolic speech," but a preference for a style or fashion. School authority clearly took precedence over fashion. But the Tinkers were not obeying the dictates of fashion but of morality when they put on their armbands. The armbands were not just fabric but a message. Thus the first thing that Abe Fortas decided to say in his opinion, after recounting the history of the case, was that the wearing of armbands "was closely akin to 'pure speech,' which, we have repeatedly held, is entitled to comprehensive protection under the First Amendment."[16]

Having established that wearing the armbands was speech, Fortas needed to address the issue of whether speech could be equally protected no matter where it took place. He discovered that the answer was "no" in 1966 in *Adderley* v. *Florida*, where a few hundred college students demonstrated outside a county jail—but some broke the law by trespassing and were not protected by the First Amendment defense. The sheriff acted for security reasons in arresting the students.[17]

Fortas also referred to the 1965 case of *Cox* v. *Louisiana*. There, an ordained minister named Elton Cox had been leading a sizable group of African-American students from a local college in a peaceful protest against segregation. He told the police their plan—to sing hymns and "The Star Spangled Banner," pray, and make speeches in the square near the courthouse in Baton Rouge. The group proceeded to do so throughout the morning. At lunchtime Reverend Cox told his protesters to go to the nearby whites-only lunchrooms and buy lunch. The police warned him he had gone too far by upsetting a group of whites, and when Cox's group showed no intention of dispersing, the police set off tear gas. The next day, Cox was arrested on various charges including breach of the peace. The Court held that Cox was deprived of his rights of free speech and free assembly.[18] Justice Black had written a concurrence to clarify that the plaintiffs had won only because they were in a town square that was open for public uses such as protests:

> The First and Fourteenth Amendments, I think, take away from government, state and federal, all power to restrict freedom of speech, press, and assembly where people have a right to be for such purposes. This does not mean, however, that these amendments also grant a constitutional right to [picket anywhere one wants to]. [Were] the law otherwise, people on the streets, in their homes and anywhere else could be compelled to

listen against their will to speakers they did not want to hear.[19]

This could easily apply to the *Tinker* case. Students who, for various reasons, did not want to be confronted with the message of the armbands could certainly say they were forced to see them. Justice Black was carving out exceptions to his absolute guarantee of freedom of expression. They were very sensible ones at that. Was the schoolroom any different from the town square? Was it more like a home, or more like a public forum? Justice Fortas decided this way:

> First Amendment rights, applied in the light of the special characteristics of the school environment, are available to teachers and students. It can hardly be argued that either students or teachers shed their constitutional rights to freedom of speech or expression at the schoolhouse gate.[20]

Why Justice Fortas included teachers in his opinion is not clear. Nothing in the *Tinker* facts required him to do so. But it reinforces the notion of the schoolroom as a miniature world, with both adults and young people in it. If students like the Tinkers were where they were supposed to be (indeed, required to be), then they should have full free speech rights as long as they were not disruptive.

Fortas even followed the plaintiffs' idealistic

arguments that government must teach students by example that free speech is important. The fact that schools are "educating the young for citizenship is reason for scrupulous protection of Constitutional freedoms of the individual, if we are not to strangle the free mind at its source and teach youth to discount important principles of our government. . . ."[21]

But now it was time to balance these ideals with the realities of the school day. The public school also has a "right," one might say, to be allowed to do what it was created to do: educate the students entrusted to it. Justice Fortas introduced the topic this way: "Our problem lies in the area where students in the exercise of First Amendment rights collide with the rules of school authorities."[22]

Fortas said there was "no evidence whatever" that there was any interference, actual or just beginning,

> with the schools' work or of collision with the rights of other students to be secure and to be let alone. . . . There is no indication that . . . any class was disrupted. Outside the classrooms, a few students made hostile remarks to the children wearing armbands, but there were no threats or acts of violence on school premises. . . [It is true that school authorities] feared a disturbance from the wearing of the armbands. But, in our system, undifferentiated fear or apprehension of disturbance is not enough to overcome the right to freedom of expression. Any departure from absolute regimentation may cause trouble. Any variation from

the majority's opinion may inspire fear. Any word spoken, in class, or in the lunchroom, or on the campus, that deviates from the view of another person may start an argument or cause a disturbance. But our Constitution says we must take this risk. . . .[23]

Justice Fortas even quoted the same words from an earlier opinion that the Tinkers had quoted in their brief: "The classroom is peculiarly the 'marketplace of ideas.' The Nation's future depends upon leaders trained through wide exposure to that robust exchange of ideas which discovers truth 'out of a multitude of tongues, [rather] than through any kind of authoritative selection.'"[24]

Justice Warren's concern about evenhandedness was included, too. "It is also relevant," Fortas wrote, "that the school authorities did not purport [claim] to prohibit the wearing of all symbols of political or controversial significance. The record shows that students in some of the schools wore buttons relating to national political campaigns, and some even wore the Iron Cross, traditionally a symbol of Nazism. The order prohibiting the wearing of armbands did not extend to these." Only the armband was "singled out for prohibition."[25]

"[W]e do not confine the permissible exercise of First Amendment rights to a telephone booth . . . or to supervised and ordained discussion in a school

Chief Justice Earl Warren is shown here at his desk.

classroom," Fortas declared. Observing that personal intercommunication among students is a significant activity of schools, Fortas stated that "A student's rights, therefore, do not embrace merely the classroom hours. When he is in the cafeteria, or on the playing field, or on the campus during the authorized hours, he may express his opinions, even on controversial subjects like the conflict in Vietnam, if he does so without 'materially and substantially interfer[ing] with the requirements of appropriate discipline in the operation of the school' and without colliding with the rights of others."[26] There he utilized the words of *Burnside* v. *Byars*, a case the Tinkers and the *amicus curiae* had relied upon heavily.

At that point Fortas expanded his ruling beyond the point of agreement with some of the other Justices. For instance, he declared, "Students in school as well as out of school are 'persons' under our Constitution. They are possessed of fundamental rights which the State must respect, just as they themselves must respect their obligations to the State. . . . In the absence of a specific showing of constitutionally valid reasons to regulate their speech, students are entitled to freedom of expression of their views."[27] This clear statement that Fortas did not see the child speaker as any different than the adult was not well supported with authority, and

Justice Stewart added his reply at the end of the opinion in his concurrence: "I cannot share the Court's [the majority opinion is referred to as that of 'the Court'] uncritical assumption that . . . the First Amendment rights of children are co-extensive with those of adults. . . . [A]t least in some precisely delineated areas, a child . . . is not possessed of that full capacity for individual choice which is the presupposition of First Amendment guarantees."[28]

Justice White also backed off from the sweeping language of the Fortas opinion, noting that conduct is not always as protectable by the First Amendment as speech is, and that perhaps the analysis in *Burnside* v. *Byars*, cited by both the Tinkers and Justice Fortas, was faulty. He was most likely referring to the placing of the burden of proof upon the school to show an actual material disruption or substantial disorder or invasion of the rights of others. As mentioned in Chapter 3, Fortas was inclined from the beginning to handle the case in this way. The side with the burden of proof must produce the evidence first. If that side cannot bring forth enough evidence, the other side does not even have to put on a case. Proving that actual substantial disorder was caused by a particular deed could be rather hard to do. It also might risk the safety of pupils to wait till actual disruption had happened. But this was now the law.

Justice Harlan dissented. The other Justices mentioned wrote concurrences, meaning they agreed with the result even if they did not agree with the majority's reasoning. A dissent is an opinion that disagrees with the result. Sometimes dissents are quoted more than majority opinions and even become the majority opinion in future years. Dissents may attack every point of the majority ruling, or just one. Harlan's dissent was short.

While conceding that public schools were not exempt from the First Amendment's requirements, he said, ". . . school officials should be accorded the widest authority in maintaining discipline and good order in their institutions. . . . I would, in cases like this, cast upon those complaining the burden of showing that a particular school measure was motivated by other than legitimate school concerns—for example, a desire to prohibit the expression of an unpopular point of view, while permitting expression of the dominant opinion."[29] For example, in *Tinker*, the plaintiffs would have had to show that some school officials did not like the students' anti-Vietnam stance and were intentionally trying to stifle it.

But it was Justice Hugo Black who most strenuously objected to Fortas's opinion. Black had two main problems with the case. One was that the Supreme Court should not second-guess school boards, and the other was that allowing the armbands would open a floodgate of wild behavior from students. Let us examine these views more closely.

First, Black commented rather sarcastically that "The Court's holding in this case ushers in what I deem to be an entirely new era in which the power to control pupils by the elected 'officials of state supported public schools' . . . is in ultimate effect transferred to the Supreme Court."[30] Indeed, it is true that since *Tinker,* lawsuits accusing schools of civil rights violations have affected more and more schools, draining them of funds, and, sometimes, creativity.

Second, the dissenting Justice Black referred back to the original question that was presented to the Supreme Court: whether schools could prohibit "symbols of political views within school premises where the symbols are not disruptive of school discipline or decorum." Justice Black disputed the assumption that everyone had made until then—that no disruption was taking place at the Tinkers' schools due to their armbands. He wrote,

> Even a casual reading of the record shows that this armband did divert students' minds from their regular lessons, and that talk, comments, etc., made John Tinker "self-conscious" in attending school with

his armband.

While the absence of obscene remarks or boisterous and loud disorder perhaps justifies the Court's statement that the few armband students did not actually 'disrupt' the classwork, I think the record overwhelmingly shows that the armbands did exactly what the elected school officials and principals foresaw they would, that is, took the students' minds off their classwork and diverted them to thoughts about the highly emotional subject of the Vietnam war.[31]

He returned to his sarcastic tone in arguing that students are not "sent to the schools at public expense to broadcast political or any other views to educate and inform the public."[32] But his words seemed tinged with compassion when he went on to say, "Of course students, like other people, cannot concentrate on lesser issues when black armbands are being ostentatiously displayed in their presence to call attention to the wounded and dead of the war, some of the wounded and dead being their friends and neighbors."[33]

Finally, he predicted doom for the country as a result of Fortas's ruling. Students would become "willing to defy their teachers or practically all orders. This is the more unfortunate for the schools since groups of students all over the land are already running loose, conducting break-ins, sit-ins, lie-ins, and smash-ins." Justice Black once again turned sour. "This case . . . subjects all the public schools in the country to the whims and caprices of their loudest-mouthed, but maybe not their brightest, students. I, for one, am not fully persuaded that school pupils are wise enough, even with this Court's expert help from Washington, to run the 23,390 public school systems in our 50 States."[34]

When the decision came out, it was received with a variety of reactions. But Fortas's majority opinion in favor of the Tinkers hardly pleased anyone. "Few [of those who favored law and order] seemed to realize that he agreed with them that in many situations state interests might outweigh First Amendment rights." School officials said that, thanks to "you and your buddies on the court" . . . 'the highest court' has once again poked its nose into a matter which is not its business at all." Students would soon be wearing signs inviting others to "Join Abe Fortas and the S.D.S."[35] "The [other side] wanted no part of Fortas either," though.[36] He and his liberal Brethren were seen as not going far enough. ". . . [T]he changes Fortas and others had brought about . . . seemed to have sparked radicalism. Perhaps they had been insufficient. Alternatively, perhaps their reforms had been so successful that they had stimulated [one group of people] with visions of what might be possible at the same time that they mobilized [another group] by threatening the traditional vision of the good society."[37]

For Mary Beth Tinker (shown here), the *Tinker* case created a lot of publicity that made it difficult to be just like everyone else.

Not long after *Tinker* was published, Fortas wrote to an old friend saying he hoped with his booklet "Concerning Dissent and Civil Disobedience" to provide teachers with a "constructive" and "reasoned . . . basis upon which they could communicate with their students."[38] "That also seemed to be his aim in *Tinker* and in a subsequent concurrence in which he upheld the suspension of college students who had been engaged in an 'agressive and violent demonstration and not in a peaceful, nondisruptive expression such as was involved in *Tinker.*'"[39]

As attentive to the schools as he had wanted to be, he certainly did not please the school district's attorney, Allan Herrick. "He grieved over the decision," his daughter relates.[40] "I don't think the result would be the same today," Herrick's partner speculates.[41] However, Melvin Wulf, counsel for the other side, contends that it would.[42] We will examine the cases since *Tinker* in the next chapter, but for the Tinker family, the final burst of publicity brought their ordeal to an end. "I just wanted to put it out of my mind," Mary Beth Tinker said. "I didn't want to be a big star, because I was a teenager. Teenagers never want to stand out in a crowd. They just want to blend in. It was kind of a rough time when it broke."[43]

6

The Impact of the Decision

The *Tinker* decision was part of a cluster of cases about war protest. Not all arose at schools. But *Tinker* has had a lasting influence upon free speech law far beyond the limits of war protest.

When someone wants to see other cases where a specific Supreme Court case is mentioned, it is possible to look up those references in a book of "citations." When we look up *Tinker* v. *Des Moines*, we see column after column of cases that cite it. There are four phrases from *Tinker* that we see quoted over and over again.

The first is that a mere "undifferentiated [vague] fear" that disruption might happen is not enough reason to forbid speech.[1] This principle is used to avoid a "prior restraint" on speech, which amounts to unlawful censorship of speech before it is made. Another is that the rights afforded to us by the First Amendment must be "applied in light of the special characteristics of the school environment."[2] That phrase, sometimes with the word "school" omitted, forms the basis for limiting First Amendment rights in certain situations. When the Court is willing to do this, it often relies on the test for behavior that Justice Fortas created: whether it "materially disrupts classwork or involves substantial disorder or invasion of the rights of others."[3] Courts are not interested in using the First Amendment to protect wrongdoing. Finally, the principle that neither "student[s] or teachers shed their constitutional rights to freedom of speech or expression at the schoolhouse gate" has been the foundation for guaranteeing free speech at school.[4]

On March 10, 1969, only a month after *Tinker,* the Supreme Court denied certiorari on another student protest case. In *Barker* v. *Hardway,* Justice Fortas was careful to point out that in this case, "[t]he petitioners were suspended from college not for expressing their opinions on a matter of substance, but for violent and destructive interference with the rights of others. . . ."[5] He contrasted these facts with the Tinkers' "peaceful, nondisruptive expression. . . ."[6]

In 1971 Melvin Wulf, who had been so effective in the *Tinker* case, returned with another free speech case, *Healy* v. *James*.[7] It involved a group at a college that wanted to form a chapter of Students for a Democratic Society, or S.D.S. The matter went all the way to President James, administrator for the school, and he supported the decision to deny the group official recognition on campus. The Supreme Court looked carefully at the testimony given by the students about their group. It was feared by some that this group might become violent, as other S.D.S. chapters sometimes had.[8] One of the interchanges in the record went like this:

> **Q:** Could you envision the S.D.S. interrupting a class?
>
> **A:** Impossible for me to say.[9]

The Supreme Court decided that that answer could be interpreted to mean that the students did not intend to abide by the rules of the university. Any group that did not, could not be a recognized campus group. So the Supreme Court remanded the case, or sent it back to the trial court for clarification of that issue. It said that unless the testimony was clear that the students planned disruption, an "undifferentiated fear" of disturbance was keeping the students from enjoying their freedom of speech.[10]

Healy also discussed another important First Amendment right—the freedom of association. That refers to our freedom to meet together without interference from the government. The group in the case was not allowed to hold a meeting in the campus coffee shop because it was not an approved group. The Court was as displeased with this as with the free speech issue. "There can be no doubt," said the new Justice Powell, "that denial of official recognition . . . burdens or abridges that associational right."[11] Remember that the protest in the *Tinker* case basically started with a meeting. Free speech and free association are closely related rights.

In 1971 a case came out that involved draft protest. This one arose not in a school but in a courthouse. A man wore a jacket that had a crude saying against the draft into the courthouse. He said the saying on the jacket expressed the depth of his feelings against the Vietnam War and the draft. The jacket did not cause any commotion, and its wearer was guilty of no threats or violence. Justice Harlan said that prosecuting the defendant for the choice of words was wrong, and that the Court favored "putting the decision as to what views shall be voiced largely into the hands of each of us."[12]

In 1986 a high school student who gave a

controversial speech launched our next case. Matthew Fraser nominated his friend Jeff for class officer at an assembly. The problem was that the speech was full of sexual references. "Some students," the Court noted, "hooted and yelled; some by gestures graphically simulated the sexual activities pointedly alluded [referred] to in respondent's speech. Other students appeared to be bewildered and embarrassed by the speech. One teacher reported that on the day following the speech, she found it necessary to forgo a portion of the scheduled class lesson in order to discuss the speech with the class."[13]

A school rule stated, "Conduct which materially and substantially interferes with the educational process is prohibited, including the use of obscene, pro-fane language or gestures."[14] The morning after the assembly, Fraser was suspended and was told that he could not speak at graduation as planned. He sued, say-ing his speech was protected by the First Amendment. The Supreme Court acknowleged that though students do not shed their free speech rights at the schoolhouse gate, "[t]he undoubted freedom to advocate [advance] unpopular and controversial views in schools and class-rooms must be balanced against the society's counter-vailing interest in teaching students the boundaries of socially appropriate behavior."[15] Thus it was all right for the school to have the rule it did, and to enforce it. "The pervasive [continuous] sexual innuendo in Fraser's speech was plainly offensive to both teachers and students—indeed to any mature person. By glorifying male sexuality, and in its verbal content, the speech was acutely insulting to girl students."[16] The Court felt that the Tinkers' "speech" had been different in that theirs was not "speech or action that intrudes on the work of the schools or the rights of other students."[17]

It was not long before a school newspaper case was argued before the Supreme Court. It was *Hazelwood School District* v. *Kuhlmeier,* and it all started in 1988, in a journalism class in the St. Louis area.

The students in charge of the *Spectrum,* the journalism class newspaper, at Hazelwood East High School, put together the final regular issue. It was six pages, as the others usually had been. Two of these pages were devoted to articles that became the source of the litigation. One covered the sexual and pregnancy experiences of three girls at the high school. Another discussed the impact of divorce on students, and included quotes from students about their own parents' breakups.

The principal, Dr. Robert Reynolds, reviewed the paper and felt that the two articles had to be changed before the school could print them. In the first, the identities of the girls were not well concealed to ensure privacy. The article contained material that Reynolds considered unsuitable for the younger students in the school. In the other, critical comments made about the students' parents called for at least a notification of the people discussed and a chance for them to respond. Dr. Reynolds tells the story: "The journalism teacher was on the phone from the printer to get my go-ahead . . . But the articles were not up to journalistic standards. I was in a pickle, having to make an instant decision—the printer had his finger on the button. So I made the call: the two articles would not run."[18] A four-page paper, he felt, was better than none. The journalism students were incensed with this move and photocopied the articles and handed them out at school. Dr. Reynolds knew of this but did not stop them. That was a matter of their own private expression, he felt. But the newspaper was the school's responsibility. Three newspaper staff members eventually filed suit for violation of their free speech rights. The suit did not affect the atmosphere at school much. "These were good kids—they were student leaders. Journalism kids are," said Reynolds.[19]

Interestingly, once the case became public, a local newspaper printed the divorce article, but without any names in it. Thus the professional local editors made the same judgment call that Reynolds had—that they could be sued for libel or invasion of privacy if they did not take some measures to leave personal identities out.[20]

While acknowledging that the students had not "shed their constitutional rights . . . at the schoolhouse gate, [w]e have nonetheless recognized that the First Amendment rights of students in the public schools 'are not automatically coextensive [equal] with the rights of adults in other settings.'"[21] This was something the majority in *Tinker* had not said, though Justice Stewart had suggested the idea in his concurrence as did Black in his dissent. It somewhat limits the impact of *Tinker*, because it allows the school to interfere with a student's expression even if the expression does not cause disruption. In the *Hazelwood* case, no one was saying the articles were creating a disturbance at school. The school was simply saying that it had a right to control the standards of the paper because it was a school-sponsored activity. The Court agreed. "Hence, a school may in its capacity as publisher of a school newspaper or producer of a school play . . . [prohibit not only] speech that would 'substantially interfere with [its] work . . . or impinge upon the rights of other students' [a phrase from Tinker], but also . . .

speech that is, for example, ungrammatical, poorly written, inadequately researched, biased or prejudiced, vulgar or profane, or unsuitable for immature audiences."[22] Careful to say that the armbands were the Tinkers' own speech, the Court said that here the articles amounted to the speech of the school since they would appear in a school-sponsored publication. Thus the school could control what was said.

The case generated a fair amount of publicity. "We got offers for movie contracts," comments Reynolds. "Is this absurd or what?"[23] But he adds, "The winner in the case is scholastic journalism. Without the protection of this decision, schools all over the country would have folded their papers because they might be sued for false statements in them."[24] Without some authority to oversee the words printed, the school would not take the risk of liability for those words.

The next case we will look at is one that did not rely directly on the First Amendment. Yet it has expanded the free speech rights of students at the end of the twentieth century perhaps more than any other case. It is called *Westside Community Board of Education* v. *Mergens*.

In 1985, a high school student named Bridget Mergens went to talk to her principal. She was not in trouble—she had a suggestion. She wanted to start a

Christian club, one that would have the same privileges as the other clubs that already existed at Westside High School. Her idea was to have a group where any students who so desired could read and discuss the Bible and pray with other students. Her principal and later the school superintendent denied her request. They said that having such a club would cause the school to appear to be "establishing," or promoting, a religion. A government-funded (public) school cannot do this because one part of the First Amendment, called the Establishment Clause, says that the government cannot "establish" a state religion.

But a new law that Congress had passed made Bridget Mergens and others think differently. It was not long before a courageous young lawyer, Jay Sekulow, and the Solicitor General for the United States, Kenneth Starr, were at her side. The new law that they relied on is the Equal Access Act. This act, passed in 1984, said:

> It shall be unlawful for any public secondary school which receives Federal financial assistance and which has a limited open forum to deny equal access or a fair opportunity to, or discriminate against, any students who wish to conduct a meeting within that limited open forum on the basis of the religious, political, philosophical, or other content of the speech at such meetings.[25]

There continues to be much debate about whether or not prayer should be allowed in public schools. The *Mergens* case established students' rights to have religious clubs on school campuses.

"Equal access" is understood to mean the permission to advertise, seek funds, meet, and use facilities and other privileges. Mergens's position was that she should have the same access to meeting times and places and publicity that other groups had. The groups that were allowed included the Chess Club, the Subsurfers (for those interested in scuba diving), two service clubs, the National Honor Society, the Photography Club, and the Student Advisory Board. The Supreme Court eventually held that having even one of these other clubs obligated the school to allow a Christian club too, since having any "noncurriculum-related" club creates a "limited open forum," whether the school admits it or not. Justice Sandra Day O'Connor, the first woman on the Supreme Court, wrote, "In our view, a student group directly relates to a school's curriculum if the subject matter of the group is actually taught, or will soon be taught, in a regularly offered course; if the subject matter of the group concerns the body of courses as a whole; if participation in the group is required for a particular course; or if participation in the group results in academic credit."[26] She looked closely at the evidence and had no trouble finding several clubs that were noncurricular, such as most listed above. Thus the school had opened a forum, and once it did, it could not discriminate on the basis of the type of speech, or content, of the club.[27]

The school had objected that it could not permit a religious club on campus because a teacher was required to sponsor each club, and having a teacher at Mergens's club meetings would appear to be school promotion of religion. The Court pointed out that Congress had thought of that and had provided that school employees could attend in a nonparticipating role.[28] As a result of this legislation and the *Mergens* case, which found that the Christian club did not violate the Establishment Clause, approximately six hundred thousand public school students are involved in religious clubs on campuses now.[29]

In *Rosenberger* v. *University of Virginia*, Ron Rosenberger was a student at the university who wanted help with funding for his publication, *Wide Awake*.[30] This was a publication with the stated purpose "to challenge Christians to live, in word and deed, according to the faith they proclaim and to encourage students to consider what a personal relationship with Jesus Christ means."[31] Topics in the first issue included racism, crisis pregnancy, prayer, and reviews of religious music. Each page was marked with a cross.[32] The university gathered a mandatory fourteen-dollar student activity fee each semester from

In the case of *Rosenberger* v. *Univeristy of Virginia*, the Supreme Court decided that a religious viewpoint cannot be discriminated against in funding campus speech. Rosenberg (seated) is shown with attorney Michael McDonald outside the Supreme Court.

all full-time students at the university and a committee of students would review the requests of all organizations and publications that wanted to use some of that money to conduct activities. Rosenberger and his staff were "somewhat surprised" when the committee turned them down flat. He met with the Student Council and got nowhere—"Someone at Student Council laughed and said, 'See you in the Supreme Court,'" Rosenberger recalls. "We had no idea it would go this far. It's not like we were sue-happy. But after we'd pursued every avenue of appeal with the University, we contacted the Center for Individual Rights in Washington, D.C."[33]

Facing the Supreme Court in a lawsuit was not easy for the staff. "It was scary. A lot of people don't appeal for that reason," he says.[34]

Once in Court, the university claimed that since the amount of funds for student activities was limited, the activities closest to the educational mission of the school ought to be funded first.[35] But the *Wide Awake* staff countered that other publications that did get funding included a Muslim and a Jewish periodical, as well as publications that printed various antireligious views. To this, the university answered that those were cultural publications and did not "proselytize," or attempt to convert the reader to the author's ideology.

The trial took less than two hours, consisting mostly of documents and arguments rather than witnesses. Rosenberger himself never took the stand.[36]

Four and a half years after the original incident, the case was argued before the Supreme Court. Rosenberger attended.

He looked up at the mural around the courtroom and noticed a scene showing Moses holding the Ten Commandments. "That was the time the momentousness of it all struck me. It was exciting."[37] His attorney, Michael McConnell, began, not using any notes. To Rosenberger, Justice Scalia seemed very fiery. Justice Thomas was silent. Justice Breyer seemed very skeptical and even rolled his eyes and turned his chair away from the university's attorney. Justices O'Connor and Ginsberg asked a lot of questions. After oral arguments, Rosenberger said: "The other side seemed to be trying to evade the Constitutional issues, and the Court doesn't like evasiveness. The University was talking about money, and the Supreme Court doesn't take your one case out of a hundred to talk about money."[38]

The Supreme Court was not convinced by the university's arguments. The Court observed that topics that appeared in *Wide Awake* were the kind covered in funded publications, the only difference being the Christian viewpoint. "Viewpoint discrimination" is illegal, the Court said: "The prohibited perspective, not the general subject matter, resulted in the refusal of funds. . . .[T]he University may not silence the expression of selected viewpoints" while permitting others.[39] Justice Kennedy, writing for the majority, in 1995, also took note that *Wide Awake* "did not seek a subsidy because of its Christian editorial viewpoint; it sought funding as a student journal, which it was."[40] He was referring to one of the categories of groups which could seek payment, which was "student news, information, opinion. . . ."[41]

As the term of Court drew to a close, Ron Rosenberger began to spend more and more time at the Court, hoping to hear news of his case. On the last possible day, the ruling favoring his publication was announced.

Rosenberger, who graduated before the case reached the Supreme Court, now trains high-school and college-level students in how to start independent student publications with the Leadership Institute in Arlington, Virginia. The University of Virginia has changed its policy: "The first University-financed issue of *Wide Awake* came out in November of 1995."[42]

What has become of the people in the *Tinker* case? The Tinkers' mother teaches peace studies at her local college. Mrs. Tinker says, "We're going to have to find a way to educate our leaders and our people on how to make peace."[43] Reverend Tinker has passed away. John Tinker works as a computer programmer. He comments, "We won our case, but I think there are many good cases that lose. Pursuing change through the legal system can work, but it's not perfect, so people should pay attention to whether our governmental system is working, and use it where it is working. . . . People often introduce themselves to me and say, 'You don't know me, but I know about your case.' It has given me the belief that a person has the ability to affect the world."[44] He also agrees with Mary Gefe, who was on the school board and voted against the armbands, when she says, "You need to think about what you say and its impact on someone else."[45] Dick Moberly has continued to teach in Des Moines for thirty-five years. He remembers, "I was dumbfounded the day I was called into the principal's office and served a paper by a federal officer. According to the law, since I was named as a defendant in the case, I couldn't leave the state without the Court's permission. I felt locked into my state, sort of under house arrest."[46] When asked what he would say to young people today about freedom of speech, he says, "I want freedom of speech with responsibility. How to curb it to protect innocent people is difficult."[47]

Mary Beth Tinker is shown here with her mom. Mrs. Tinker now teaches at her local college.

Chris Eckhardt recalls when he heard they had won. "I was in my dorm room [at college]. . . . A reporter called with the news. I was ecstatic. It was a proud day in America for the First Amendment. . . . [I]f the cause is just, you can use the system and make a better society."[48] He now works to enforce child support payments.

Mary Beth Tinker is a mother, and says, "I consider myself an advocate for children." She works as a nurse at a children's hospital and has cared for veterans, some of whom fought in Vietnam. She clarifies that she "never really was a pacifist. I was against Vietnam, but I think there are cases when you have to take up arms."[49] But she also says, "I'm really proud that we had a part in ending the . . . Vietnam War."[50]

Questions for Discussion

1. The *Tinker* case was decided in part on the issue of whether actual disruption would result from a particular type of expression. Should it matter if other students are merely offended by the expression? Consider for example this passage from Justice Black's dissent: "Of course students, like other people, cannot concentrate on lesser issues when black armbands are being ostentatiously displayed in their presence to call attention to the wounded and dead of the war, some of the wounded and dead being their friends and neighbors." Should a person whose father or brother is off at war have to be subjected to antiwar protests from others? Among adults, the answer is yes, but do children or teens need more protection at school? Is the concern about violence at school so much greater today that the Court might rule differently now?

2. Supreme Court Justice Lewis F. Powell, Jr., wrote, "Our decisions concern the liberty, property, and even

the lives of litigants. There can be no posturing among us, and no thought of tomorrow's headlines." What kinds of headlines in 1968 might have made an impartial decision difficult for the *Tinker* Court?

3. In his book, *Taking Liberties*, Alan Dershowitz says, "I hereby offer five hundred dollars of my own to any group of responsible students at the Hazelwood East High School who are prepared to continue in the tradition of Cathy Kuhlmeier and her fellow editors who challenged censorship. If you want to start an independent newspaper reporting on matters of interest to the students, my small contribution will probably cover the printing cost for two or three times. Then you're on your own. I will not demand the right to see copy in advance. I am confident that you will exercise your freedom responsibly." Why did he limit his offer to "responsible students"? What would you like to put in such a paper? Who would you want to read it?

4. How important to winning the *Tinker* case was the fact that the Tinkers were otherwise cooperative students who were making good grades? What steps did they take that Ron Rosenberger also took? (See Chapters 1 and 7.)

5. Is your school a public or private school? Do the cases covered in this book have anything to say about private schools? Which rulings are or should be limited to public schools? In some ways, students have greater freedom in public schools and in others they have less. Explain.

6. Think about the following situations and discuss whether people should have a right to express these kinds of things:
> —lies
> —private information that has been held in trust about someone else
> —threats or "fighting words"
> —something that could spread a panic, such as a rumor
> —a belief that one's ideas are true and everyone else is wrong
> —comments that others are sure to find offensive or will hurt their feelings

(Taken in part from Dale Greenwald's "Liberty" in *Lawyer's Resource Manual*, Oklahoma City: Oklahoma Bar Association, reprinted from *Constitutional Update: Liberty*, a publication of the American Bar Association Special Committee on Youth Education for Citizenship.) (Case law currently protects the last two, and sometimes the second, items.)

Chapter Notes

Chapter 1

1. Peter Irons and Stephanie Guitton, eds., *May It Please the Court* (New York: The New Press, 1993), p. 129.

2. *Tinker* v. *Des Moines Independent Community School District*, 393 U.S. 503, (1969), Record on Appeal of Examinations of Witnesses, p. 54.

3. Ibid., p. 16.

4. Ibid., p. 22.

5. Ibid., p. 24.

6. Jack Magarrell, *Des Moines Register*, December 15, 1965, quoted in Doreen Rappaport, *Tinker* vs. *Des Moines: Student Rights on Trial* (New York: HarperCollins, 1996), p. 77.

7. *Tinker*, Record, p. 26.

8. Ibid., p. 18.

9. Ibid., pp. 55-56.

10. Ibid., p. 52.

11. D. Elton Trueblood, *The People Called Quakers* (New York: Harper and Row, 1966), p. 190.

12. *Tinker*, Record, p. 44.

13. Trueblood, p. 207.

14. James Haskins, *The Methodists* (New York: Hippocrene Books, 1992), p. 122.

15. Interview with Lorena Jeanne Tinker, June 4, 1996.

16. *Tinker*, Record, p. 35.

17. Ibid., p. 26.

18. *Tinker*, Record, Petitioner's Brief, p. 5, note 2.

19. Ibid.

20. Irons and Guitton, p. 123.

21. *Tinker*, Record on Appeal of Examination of Witnesses, p. 49.

22. Rappaport, p. 24.

23. Ibid., p. 23.

24. Interview with Lorena Jeanne Tinker, June 4, 1996.

25. Rappaport, p. 24.

Chapter 2

1. George Lipsitz, "Who'll Stop the Rain?" *The Sixties: From Memory to History*, ed. David Farber (Chapel Hill: University of North Carolina Press, 1994), p. 209.

2. Henry J. Abraham, *Justices and Presidents* (New York: Oxford University Press, 1974), p. 252.

3. Richard Goodwin, *Remembering America* (Boston: Little, Brown, 1988), p. 369.

4. Ibid., pp. 370-371.

5. David Halberstam, *The Best and the Brightest* (New York: Random House, 1972), pp. 207, 250, 259-60.

6. Walter La Feber, *The American Age* (New York: W. W. Norton and Co., 1989), p. 564.

7. Goodwin, p. 371 and Halberstam, pp. 96, 102, 300.

8. Goodwin, p. 355.

9. Ibid., p. 287.

10. Ibid., p. 374.

11. Halberstam, p. 354.

12. Lipsitz, p. 212.

13. Ibid.

14. Ibid., p. 209.

15. Irwin Unger and Debi Unger, *Turning Point: 1968* (New York: Charles Scribner's Sons, 1988), pp. 165-167.

16. "Personal Glimpses," *Reader's Digest*, September, 1995, p. 87.

17. Lipsitz, p. 222.

18. Ronald Berman, *America in the Sixties: an Intellectual History* (New York: The Free Press, 1968), pp. 80-81, and Unger, pp. 260-286, 427.

19. Unger, p. 261.

20. Ibid., p. 286.

21. Ibid., p. 285.

22. Ibid., p. 265.

23. Ibid.

24. Ibid., p. 286.

25. Ibid., pp. 270-271.

26. Abe Peck, *Uncovering the Sixties: The Life and Times of the Underground Press* (New York: Pantheon, 1985), p. 118.

27. Kenneth Cmiel, "The Politics of Civility," *The Sixties: From Memory to History*, ed. David Farber (Chapel Hill: University of North Carolina Press, 1994), p. 273.

28. Lewis Chester, Godfrey Hodgson, and Bruce Page, *An American Melodrama: The Presidential Campaign of 1968* (New York: Viking, 1969), p. 497.

29. Margaret Hope Bacon, *Let This Life Speak: The Legacy of Henry Joel Cadbury* (Philadelphia: University of Pennsylvania Press, 1987), p. 135.

30. Ibid., p. 68.

31. Unger, pp. 438-439.

32. Ibid., pp. 443-446.

33. Martin A. Lee and Bruce Shlain, *Acid Dreams: The CIA and the Sixties Rebellion* (New York: Grove, 1985), p. 160.

34. Jerry Rubin, *Do It!* (New York: Simon and Schuster, 1970), p. 113.

35. Berman, p. 86.

36. "The Turned-on, Tuned-in World of Hippie Capitalists," *Cosmopolitan*, May 1970, p. 155.

37. Lipsitz, p. 208.

38. Unger, p. 345.

39. Cmiel, pp. 276-277.

40. David Farber, "The Silent Majority," p. 298.

41. Robert Coles, *The Middle Americans: Proud and Uncertain* (Boston: Little, Brown, 1971), p. 45.

42. Myra MacPherson, *Long Time Passing: Vietnam and the Haunted Generation* (New York: Doubleday, 1984), p. 555.

43. Unger, p. 192.

44. Ibid., p. 161.

45. Theodore H. White, *The Making of the President* (New York: Atheneum Publishers), 1965, p. 246.

46. Unger, p. 87.

47. Ibid., p. 109.

48. Ibid., pp. 116-123.

49. Lyndon Baynes Johnson, *The Vantage Point: Perspectives of the Presidency, 1963-1969* (New York: Holt, Rinehart, and Winston, 1971), p. 427.

50. Thomas W. Pauken, *The Thirty Years War: The Politics of the Sixties Generation* (Ottawa, Ill.: Jameson Books, Inc., 1995), p. 85.

51. MacPherson, p. 154.

52. Ibid., p. 622.

Chapter 3

1. Federal Civil Rights Act of 1871, C. 22, Section 1, 17 Stat. 13 (1871).

2. Steven H. Steinglass, *Section 1983 Litigation in State Courts* (New York: Clark Boardman Co., 1988), Section 2.2a, p. 2-2.

3. Ibid.

4. Interview with Herschel G. Langdon, one of the attorneys representing the school district and previously a partner of the late Allan H. Herrick, August 28, 1995.

5. Ibid.

6. Docket entries in *John F. Tinker et al.* v. *Des Moines Independent Community School District et al.*, District Court Civil No. 7-1810-C (1), p. 2, 1966.

7. *Gobitis* v. *Minersville School District*, 310 U.S. 586 (1940).

8. 363 F. 2d 744 (5th Cir. 1966).

9. Ibid., p. 748.

10. Ibid.

11. *Blackwell* v. *Issaquena County Board of Education*, 363 F. 2d 749 (5th Cir. 1966).

12. Ibid., p. 752.

13. Ibid., p. 754.

14. *Tinker* v. *Des Moines Independent Community School District*, 393 U. S. 503 (1969), Record on Appeal of Examinations of Witnesses, p. 42.

15. Peter Irons, *Brennan v. Rehnquist: The Battle for the Constitution* (New York: Alfred A. Knopf, 1994), p. 89.

16. *Tinker*, Record, p. 44.

17. Ibid., p. 22.

18. Ibid., p. 8a.

19. Laura Kalman, *Abe Fortas: A Biography* (New Haven: Yale University Press, 1990), p. 287.

20. *Tinker*, Petitioner's Brief on Appeal, p. 22.

21. Irons, pp. 88-89.

22. *Tinker* v. *Des Moines*, 258 F. Supp. at 973.

23. Interview with Melvin Wulf, October 24, 1995.

24. Interview with Mrs. Robert Henry, August 30, 1995.

25. Irwin Unger and Debi Unger, *Turning Point: 1968* (New York: Charles Scribners' Sons, 1988), p. 281.

26. Peter Irons and Stephanie Guitton, eds., *May It Please the Court* (New York: City University of New York: 1993), p. 129.

27. Thomas W. Pauken, *The Thirty Years War: The Politics of the Sixties Generation* (Ottawa, Ill.: Jameson Books, Inc., 1995), p. 104.

28. Irons and Guitton, p. 122.

29. Kalman, p. 287.

30. Ibid., quoting from a note written on a memo prepared by Fortas's clerk, Peter Zimroth, February 14, 1968, AFSC.

31. Brief of *Amicus*, *Tinker* v. *Des Moines*.

32. 319 U.S. 624, 1943.

33. Ibid., p. 635.

34. *Tinker*, Brief of Petitioners, p. 10.

35. *United States* v. *O'Brien*, 391 U.S. 367, 1968; *Adderley* v. *Florida*, 385 U.S. 39, 1967.

36. *Tinker*, Brief of Petitioners, p. 25.

37. Ibid., p. 13.

38. *Tinker*, Brief of Respondents, Proposition I.

39. Ibid.

Chapter 4

1. Bernard Schwartz, "Earl Warren," *The Supreme Court Justices,* ed. Clare Cushman (Washington, D.C.: Congressional Quarterly, Inc., 1993), p. 440.

2. *Gideon* v. *Wainwright,* 372 U.S. 335, 1963.

3. Clare Cushman, "Abe Fortas," *The Supreme Court Justices,* p. 474.

4. *Newsweek,* August 9, 1965, unpaged.

5. Henry J. Abraham, *Justices and Presidents* (New York: Oxford University Press, 1974), p. 263; Bruce Allen Murphy, *Fortas: The Rise and Ruin of a Supreme Court Justice* (New York: William Morrow and Co., Inc., 1988), p. 587.

6. Murphy, p. 593.

7. Earl Warren, *The Memoirs of Earl Warren* (Garden City, N.Y.: Doubleday and Company, Inc., 1977), p. 17.

8. Ibid., p. 21.

9. Ibid., pp. 17, 24-27.

10. Ibid., pp. 18, 28.

11. Ibid., p. 7.

12. Harvey Fireside and Sarah Betsy Fuller, *Brown v. Board of Education: Equal Schooling for All* (Hillside, N.J.: Enslow Publishers, Inc., 1994), pp. 74-75.

13. *The Supreme Court: Justice and the Law* (Washington, D.C.: Congressional Quarterly, January 1974), p. 63.

14. Murphy, p. 588.

15. *The Supreme Court: Justice and the Law,* p. 62.

16. Fireside and Fuller, pp. 56-59.

17. Dennis J. Hutchinson, "Byron White," *The Supreme Court Justices,* ed. Clare Cushman, p. 464.

18. Ibid., p. 463.

19. Ibid., p. 465.

20. Abraham, pp. 250-251.

21. *The Supreme Court: Justice and the Law*, p. 63.

22. *Jacobellis* v. *Ohio*, 378 U.S. 184, 197,(1964), concurrence.

23. Sidney H. Asch, *The Supreme Court and Its Great Justices*, (New York: Arco Publishing Co., Inc., 1971), p. 220.

24. Nathan Lewin, "John Marshall Harlan," *The Supreme Court Justices*, ed. Clare Cushman, p. 443.

25. *Street* v. *New York*, 394 U.S. 576 (1969).

26. Lewin, p. 445.

27. *The Oxford Companion to the Supreme Court of the United States*, ed. Kermit Hall (New York: Oxford University Press, 1992), p. 299.

28. Peter Irons, *Brennan v. Rehnquist: The Battle for the Constitution* (New York: Alfred A. Knopf, 1994), p. 89.

29. Peter Irons and Stephanie Guitton, eds., *May It Please the Court* (New York: The New Press, 1993), pp. 122-126.

30. Doreen Rapppaport, *Tinker vs. Des Moines: Students Rights on Trial* (New York: Harper Collins, 1993), pp. 115-117.

31. Irons and Guitton, p. 127.

32. Ibid., pp. 127-131.

33. Hall, p. 989.

34. Lewis Powell, Jr., "Myths and Misconceptions about the Supreme Court," *Journal of the American Bar Association*, Vol. 61, November 1975, p. 1344.

35. Laura Kalman, *Abe Fortas: A Biography* (New Haven: Yale Univeristy Press, 1990), p. 288.

36. Bernard Schwartz, *Super Chief: Earl Warren and His Supreme Court—A Judicial Biography* (New York: New York University Press, 1983), pp. 736-737.

37. Bernard Schwartz, *The Supreme Court Justices*, ed. Clare Cushman, p. 440.

Chapter 5

1. *United States* v. *O'Brien,* 391 U.S. 367, (1968) p. 369.
2. Ibid., p. 370.
3. Ibid., p. 381.
4. *Gobitis* v. *Minersville School District,* 310 U.S. 586, 1940, p. 598.
5. Ibid.
6. Ibid., pp. 599-600.
7. Ibid., p. 600.
8. *West Virginia Board of Education* v. *Barnette,* 319 U.S. 624, 1942, p. 630.
9. Ibid., p. 632.
10. Ibid., p. 638.
11. *Tinker* v. *Des Moines Independent Community School District,* 393 U.S. 503, 508, (1969).
12. *Ferrell* v. *Dallas Independent School District,* 392 F. 2d 697, 698 (5th Circuit 1968).
13. Ibid., p. 700.
14. Ibid., p. 701.
15. Ibid.
16. *Tinker,* p. 506.
17. *Adderley* v. *Florida,* 385 U.S. 39 (1966).
18. *Cox* v. *Louisiana,* 379 U.S. 536 (1965).
19. Ibid., p. 578.
20. *Tinker,* p. 506.
21. Ibid., p. 507, quoting *West Virginia State Board of Education* v. *Barnette,* 319 U.S. 624, 637 (1943).

22. Ibid., p. 507.

23. Ibid., p. 508.

24. Ibid., p. 512, quoting *Keyishian* v. *Board of Regents,* 385 U.S. 589, 603 (1967); *Shelton* v. *Tucker,* 364 U.S. 479, 487 (1960).

25. *Tinker,* pp. 510-511.

26. Ibid., pp. 512-513.

27. Ibid., p. 511.

28. Ibid., p. 515.

29. Ibid., p. 526.

30. Ibid., p. 515.

31. Ibid., p. 518.

32. Ibid., p. 522.

33. Ibid., p. 524.

34. Ibid., pp. 525-526.

35. Laura Kalman, *Abe Fortas: A Biography* (New Haven: Yale University Press, 1990), p. 291.

36. Ibid.

37. Ibid., p. 292.

38. Ibid., p. 289.

39. Ibid.

40. Interview with Mrs. Robert Henry, August 30, 1995.

41. Interview with Herschel G. Langdon, August 28, 1995.

42. Interview with Melvin Wulf, October 24, 1995.

43. Peter Irons, *Brennan v. Rehnquist: The Battle for the Constitution* (New York: Alfred A. Knopf, 1994), p. 89.

Chapter 6

1. *Tinker* v. *Des Moines,* 393 U.S. 503, 508 (1969).

2. Ibid., p. 506.

3. Ibid., p. 513.

4. Ibid., p. 506.

5. 394 U. S. 905, No. 901, 1969.

6. Ibid.

7. *Healy* v. *James,* 408 U.S. 169 (1971).

8. Ibid., p. 185.

9. Ibid., p. 173.

10. Ibid., p. 191.

11. Ibid., p. 181.

12. *Cohen* v. *California,* 403 U.S. 15, 24 (1971).

13. Ibid., p. 678.

14. Ibid.

15. Ibid, p. 681.

16. Ibid., p. 683.

17. Dennis J. Hutchinson, "Byron White," *The Supreme Court Justices,* p. 64.

18. Interview with Dr. Robert Reynolds, November 9, 1995.

19. Ibid.

20. Ibid.

21. *Hazelwood School District et al.* v. *Kuhlmeier et al.,* 484 U.S. 260, 266 (1988), quoting *Tinker* at 506.

22. Ibid., p. 271.

23. Interview with Dr. Robert Reynolds, November 9, 1995.

24. Ibid.

25. 20 U.S.C. Sections 4071 a and b.

26. *Westside Community Board of Education* v. *Mergens,* 496 U.S. 26 at 239 (1990).

27. Ibid., pp. 239-240.

28. Ibid., p. 252.

29. Interview with Spike Hawks, Campus Club Director, Youth America, November 21, 1995.

30. 115 Supreme Court Reporter 2510 (1995).

31. Ibid., p. 2515.

32. Ibid.

33. Interview with Ron Rosenberger, November 15, 1995.

34. Ibid.

35. Rosenberger, 115 Supreme Court Reporter 2510 (1995), p. 2519.

36. Rosenberger, Ibid.

37. Rosenberger.

38. Rosenberger.

39. Rosenberger, 115 Supreme Court Reporter 2510 (1995), pp. 2516-2517, 2519.

40. 115 Supreme Court Reporter 2510 (1995), p. 2522.

41. Ibid., p. 2514.

42. Rosenberger interview.

43. Interview with Lorena Jeanne Tinker, June 4, 1996.

44. Doreen Rappaport, *Tinker vs. Des Moines: Student Rights on Trial*, (New York: HarperCollins, 1966), pp. 140-141.

45. Ibid., p. 137.

46. Ibid., p. 139.

47. Ibid.

48. Ibid., pp. 134-135.

49. Interview with Mary Beth Tinker, June 10, 1996.

50. Peter Irons and Stephanie Guitton eds., *May It Please the Court* (New York: The New Press, 1993), p. 131.

Glossary

amicus curiae—Latin for "friend of the court." Someone not a party to the litigation who is permitted to file briefs and make arguments to the court.

brief—Legal arguments usually written by an attorney and submitted directly to the court.

capitalist—Person who believes that economic production, distribution, and exchange should be carried on chiefly by private individuals as opposed to government.

civil disobedience—Refusal to obey certain laws for the purpose of influencing public opinion, typically by nonviolent means.

Communist—Person who believes that the state owns all property; a member of a totalitarian political party.

concurrence—A judge's opinion agreeing with the majority but stating different reasons for the result.

deposition—Sworn testimony given by a witness before a court reporter prior to trial.

desegregation—A movement to include all races in public life and the rights of citizenship.

discrimination—The depriving of rights to a person or category based on impermissible classifications such as race or religion.

guru—Teacher and guide.

hearsay—A statement made by someone not a party to a lawsuit and not the person testifying, which is being used to prove that what was said is true; evidence not based on personal knowledge of the witness but just a repeating of what the witness heard.

injunction—An order to do or, more often, not do, a particular thing.

jurisdiction—Scope of authority or power of a court.

media—The press and other means of communication to the public, including television, radio, and newspapers.

pacifism—Opposition to war and violence.

R.O.T.C.—Reserve Officer Training Corps; a program run by various branches of the American military offered in some schools to expose students to the military and provide training in discipline and leadership skills.

truce—A temporary or permanent end to fighting.

writ of certiorari—An order from an appellate court to certify as accurate the record in a case that the lower court heard and sent to the higher court for review.

Further Reading

Younger Readers

Hakim, Joy. *The History of Us, Vol. 10: All the People.* New York: Oxford University Press, 1995.

Jenkins, Steve, et al. *The Bill of Rights and You.* St. Paul, MN: West Publishing, 1990.

Lieberman, Jethro. *Free Speech, Free Press, and the Law.* New York: Lothrop, Lee and Shepard Books, 1980.

Lindop, Edmund. *The Bill of Rights and Landmark Cases.* New York: Franklin Watts, 1989.

Middleton, Harry. *LBJ: The White House Years.* New York: Harry Abrams, Publishers, 1990.

Advanced Readers

Abraham, Henry J. *Freedom and the Court.* New York: Oxford University Press, 1988.

———. *The Judiciary.* Boston: Allyn and Bacon, Inc., 1980.

Cushman, Clare, ed. *The Supreme Court Justices.* Washington, D.C.: Congressional Quarterly, Inc., 1993.

Dudley, William. *The United States Constitution*. San Diego: Greenhaven Press, Inc., 1990.

Gitlin, Todd. *The Sixties: Years of Hope, Days of Rage*. New York: Bantam, 1987.

Goodwin, Richard. *Remembering America*. Boston: Little, Brown, 1988.

Irons, Peter, and Stephanie Guitton, eds. *May It Please the Court*. New York: The New Press, 1993.

Murphy, Bruce Allen. *Fortas: The Rise and Ruin of a Supreme Court Justice*. New York: William Morrow and Company, Inc., 1988.

Rappaport, Doreen. *Tinker* vs. *Des Moines: Student Rights on Trial*. New York: Harper Collins, 1966.

Schwartz, Bernard. *Super Chief: Earl Warren and His Supreme Court—A Judicial Biography*. New York: New York University Press, 1983.

Sekulow, Jay Alan. *Students' Rights and the Public Schools*. Virginia Beach, VA.: American Center for Law and Justice, 1993.

Unger, Irwin, and Di Unger. *Turning Point: 1968*. New York: Charles Scribner's Sons, 1988.

Warren, Earl. *The Memoirs of Earl Warren*. Garden City, New York: Doubleday and Company, Inc., 1977.

Index